**Typography as well as style and
syntax determine the ways in which
texts convey meanings.**

Robert Darnton
Director of the Harvard University Library

The Book History Reader
editors David Finkelstein and Alistair McCleery

D1354111

www.graphicdesignand.com

GraphicDesign& is a pioneering publishing house dedicated to creating intelligent, vivid books that explore how graphic design connects with all other things and the value that it brings. Established by Lucienne Roberts and Rebecca Wright, GraphicDesign& partners graphic designers with experts from other fields to inform, educate, entertain and provoke – and to challenge perceptions about what and who graphic design is for.

—

Page 1: Great Expectations
a **GraphicDesign& Literature** title
[WFG& W/Y]

GraphicDesign&

Page 1:
Great Expectations

Seventy graphic solutions

Editors
Lucienne Roberts
Rebecca Wright

A **GraphicDesign&** book

First published in 2012 by
GraphicDesign&
31 Great Sutton Street
London EC1V 0NA
UK

+44 [0]20 7490 8880
info@graphicdesignand.com
www.graphicdesignand.com

978 0 9572381 0 7

Designed by
LucienneRoberts+

Printed and bound by
CPI Group (UK) Ltd,
Croydon, CR0 4YY

Distributed by
GraphicDesign&

The moral rights of the contributors
have been asserted.

© GraphicDesign& 2012

All rights reserved. No part of this
publication may be reproduced,
stored in a retrieval system or
transmitted in any form or by any
means, electronic, mechanical,
photocopying, recording or
otherwise, without permission
of the copyright holder. Any person
who does any unauthorised act
in relation to this publication may
be liable to criminal prosecution
and civil claims including (without
limitation) any claim for damages.

10 9 8 7 6 5 4 3 2 1

A CIP catalogue record for this book
is available from the British Library.

While every effort has been made
to ensure all factual, historical and
typographic information contained
in this book is correct, the publishers
wish to make clear that in some
cases the factual data available
varies according to its original source.
All reasonable attempts have been
made to trace the copyright holders
of images reproduced in this book.
If any attribution has been omitted,
the publisher will endeavour to
amend in any subsequent editions.

Contents

Book

Word

Interaction

Image

Tone

Story

Introduction
Lucienne Roberts
Rebecca Wright
Professor Robert Patten
in conversation

On GraphicDesign&

We first discussed the premise that underpins GraphicDesign& in Amsterdam, during a research trip for our book *Design Diaries: Creative Process in Graphic Design*. We had taken refuge from winter rain in the café of the Stedelijk Museum CS. We talked about the projects included in our book and enthused about how they demonstrated what graphic design does best – connect with the rest of the world – and bemoaned the fact that the essentially outward-looking nature of our profession is often not made explicit. Gradually an idea took shape. GraphicDesign&. The clue is in the name of course...

GraphicDesign& publishes books and papers exploring the symbiotic nature of graphic design practice. Graphic design is always inextricably partnered with something else and each GraphicDesign& project connects graphic design to one of a myriad of subject areas. *Page 1: Great Expectations* is a GraphicDesign& Literature title.

On *Page 1*

GraphicDesign& is concerned with how graphic design connects with the wider world so one of our core ambitions is to reach a non-design audience. A subject pairing that struck us as highly inclusive was GraphicDesign& Literature. There's currently a lot of debate within the profession about how graphic design might be defined, but for our first book we decided to stick with something most people would recognise as graphic design, once their attention was drawn to it. We've been interested for some time in exploring how type and layout affect how we read and the assumptions a reader makes when they first see a page. Many people read novels, but the influence of the typesetting and layout is arguably invisible to most. This is in part because the conventions of classical book typography, albeit often in rather diluted or bastardised form, have remained unchanged for so long.

We decided that some kind of comparative exercise using the opening text from a novel would be an accessible way to demonstrate what expectations, differences and nuances are possible via typography and design. Having established these parameters we then had to make the surprisingly difficult decision of which book to choose.

On *Great Expectations*

We initially considered approaching a writer or literary expert (and non-designer) to choose the text, but realising that their choice may be overly personal or obscure wondered if the familiarity of a well-known text would be more helpful for designer and reader alike. We considered Daniel Defoe's *Robinson Crusoe* – arguably the first novel – and *On Murder Considered as One of the Fine Arts*, an essay by Thomas de Quincey which was among the first literary texts to be available as a digitally published book. We briefly considered the merits of a contemporary 'page-turner'. This conceit really appealed conceptually but having looked at a few we were disappointed – the content often didn't lend itself to the typographic opportunities we'd anticipated.

It was perhaps inevitable that we returned to the classics, and to Charles Dickens. When we read the first page of *Great Expectations* and found that it references lettering so directly it felt absolutely right, and the realisation that it was the bicentenary of Dickens' birth in 2012 was an additional gift. One might argue that *Great Expectations* is an archetypal novel. It is certainly loved and widely known through its many reprintings and retellings, in film, on radio, on television.

On a more personal level, Dickens lived in Doughty Street, London, in a house that is now the Dickens Museum, and this is just around the corner from our studio in Clerkenwell. It was via the Dickens Museum that we discovered and made contact with US academic and Dickens Scholar in Residence Professor Robert Patten, who has generously supported our project with his time and enthusiastic expertise and whose comments we include as contextual commentary here.

Having chosen our novel, we selected an edition to use. There are many published versions of *Great Expectations*. These not only vary in layout but also in some cases in the minutiæ of punctuation and so on. We chose the Collins Classic paperback edition as our reference. Its prelims use Roman numerals and so the first page of the novel falls on page 1, a detail that appealed to the completist in us! The text also starts lower down the page than in most other versions and we thought that supplying a shorter text would give contributors greater design freedom.

On structure

Great Expectations was a novel originally published in weekly instalments, in the columns of the periodical All The Year Round and then re-set for three-volume publication. So already the novel had two print instantiations at the beginning, which is not the case with all of Charles Dickens' other fictions.

Each of these can be read differently and there are different expectations with each material and instantiation too. One might suggest that Dickens thought about Great Expectations in three different ways. He planned it, originally, for publication in monthly parts, and he continued to keep his manuscript in these parts and would renumber his pages at the beginning of each month. Each monthly part contained four instalments for All The Year Round.

Then he thought that four of those monthly parts would be a stage, and these three volumes, or three stages of Pip's 'great expectations', created a structure that allowed him to sell 1,400 copies to Moody's library, and reach a readership he hadn't really penetrated with serial parts or the one-volume novel.

Of course he published it in weekly instalments too. With a weekly instalment in particular, the story can go on and on and on, the characters can morph, there's always going to be some sort of suspense, which is going to get resolved... With a monthly part, there is a more rounded kind of staging. It's like a drama where you have exposition, complication and resolution. These parts have their own structure that are necessary to the completion of the whole, but each part should also be complete within itself.

On the brief

The brief that was set for our 70 contributing designers was to lay out the first page of *Great Expectations*. It was an invitation to test our assertion that typography affects the way in which we read a novel and an opportunity for the designers to challenge the conventions of book typography, or to work within them. We supplied the text as it appears on the first page of the current Collins Classics paperback version.

The range of interpretations fascinated us. Some contributors approached the project as if their page was the precursor to the entire novel, but many more treated the copy as display setting and clearly enjoyed the chance to challenge convention, sometimes not even relating their design to the story, or to the idea of book design. We pondered on what this might signify. Design is often said to be all about constraints and designers generally embrace them in preference to the freedom (and terror) of a totally blank page. Our brief was intentionally open, and so it wasn't surprising that our contributors welcomed the opportunity to challenge boundaries and highlight the way that designers think, test and experiment.

An important part of the brief was asking designers to write a rationale explaining their design decisions. These have proved surprisingly revealing and often run counter to expectations when you look at the work. Reading the rationales adds significantly to the experience of looking at the page layouts as they make clear the high level of detail and consideration applied in the design process.

Inevitably, various contributors approached us asking to use more or less text than we'd supplied, or show more than one option. One wanted their page 1 to be printed letterpress and tipped in... despite having a bit of the control freak about us, we conceded on many of these ideas so long as they were 'justified' in the rationales.

On typography and layout

All sorts of aspects of type and layout affect reading: the slant of letters, the spacing between letters, the leading between lines, the size of type, the style of type, flush or ragged right margins (I rather liked the ranged left, ragged right settings you showed me, eliminating distracting hyphenated words), formatting that leaves too little space in the gutter or outer margins, etc. I think introducing different fonts, or increasing/ decreasing font size, or changing the density of the printed letter on the page, or any other visual variant, can have quite an effect. Italics are sometimes used to suggest a whispering voice, or something written down rather than spoken: and some readers respond to that different type by sensing it as a different register.

I'm interested in the way the different material instantiations of the book could influence the reading or rereading of different dimensions of the book's themes and emphases, so that when the reader comes to the end, how they have read it has been partly dependent on how they were given the material 'book' to begin with.

The brief

Introduction

This is an invitation to take part in the forthcoming GraphicDesign& project and publication: *Page 1: Great Expectations*. We are asking 70 graphic designers/ typographers varying in age, background and experience, to each lay out the text of page 1 of *Great Expectations* by Charles Dickens.

This project is a typographic experiment of sorts. Free to lay out the text as you wish, this is an opportunity for you to challenge or celebrate the conventional classically derived layout of novels that still dominates today.

Published together in standard paperback format, these 70 page 1s will provide a comparative study of the effect that typography and layout have on the way that we read and interpret text and the voice that it lends to the stories we tell and read.

The cover of the brief showed page 1 of *Great Expectations* by Charles Dickens, Collins Classics, Harper Press, an imprint of HarperCollinsPublishers, 2010 edition.

Design task

Using the specification below please lay out the first page of *Great Expectations* by Charles Dickens, in a way you see fit.

Rationale

Please provide a short rationale for your layout including the choice of font and type size, in no more than 300 words.

Format
standard paperback, one colour (black)

Dimensions
one right hand page measuring 178mm x 110mm, portrait

Artwork
to be supplied as print ready pdf with crop marks

The text

Great Expectations was first published from December 1860 to August 1861 in serial form in the weekly magazine *All The Year Round* and was first published in book form in 1861. One of Dickens' best loved novels, it has been adapted for stage and screen many, many times and has never been out of print.

We are using the text from the first page of the current Collins Classics edition of *Great Expectations*. We are happy to send you a copy of the novel if you wish.

On the results

We felt simultaneously thrilled and a little overwhelmed by the breadth of responses to this brief. Initially we were going to show the work running in alphabetical order by design group or designer surname, but having looked at the layouts we started to identify groupings based upon the recurring themes that we found most interesting. The value of these became clear when we visited Robert Patten. He helped us look objectively at the designs. As we laid out the pages for him to consider, we became aware of how grouping by theme was useful for the purposes of comparison. This directly informed our decision to organise the designs within six overarching categories in the finished book. However, it's important to stress that these are not definitive (indeed some entries could be placed in more than one category) and exist only as a curatorial device that provides greater opportunity for comparison.

On first responses

Great Expectations *is a Victorian novel and there is a question as to whether the reader loses something when it is set in a contemporary typeface. I thought the setting according to grammar would have been helpful to dyslexic students, those whose first language isn't English, and readers in general who need to find ways to enter Dickens' complicated and very 'dependent-variable' grammar. I liked those settings that emphasised PIP – because both PIP and PIRRIP are palindromes, and they look funny as well. 'Pip' of course also means seed, or star.*

Something that no designer emphasised, because it's not an aspect of type, is the gravestone inscription 'Also Georgiana Wife of the Above' that would have been carved into the stone. Stones are used in lithography, but not by carving into them. Etching and engraving carve into the metal or wooden plate, so there was a chance to think about ways of printing letters that the gravestone inscription might have suggested to printers.

On how Page 1 may be used

You've produced a book that will be most useful in teaching design and for students of print culture. In addition, it would be interesting to find school teachers who are working with an assigned Dickens text – Great Expectations *if possible – and see what results they get from letting their students, who spend so much time on virtual text images, think about various material images and their effects and affects. All these steps could help to make more readers aware of the connections between 'medium' and 'message', to revive Marshal McLuhan for a moment.*

On the themes

The first category is **Book**. This encompasses designs conceived as systems to be applied to a whole book. There are lots of differences within these, even though they are ostensibly more conventional. In their rationales, the designers explain not only their thinking about font choices and typographic detailing but also how and why the text sits as it does on the page. They refer to the factors that determine their grid and reference various typographic norms that we hope readers will find interesting.

Within this category there are still designs that play with emphasis and intervention, but not so as to disrupt the reading of the text. To an extent all these contributions are experiments in design neutrality. The designers have explored layout and typography appropriate for a nineteenth-century text. Some argue that a modernist approach renders the text most accessible and open to unprejudiced interpretation. Others chose typefaces that were more contemporaneous to the text and approached their layouts as modern reworkings of a classical book page.

The second grouping is **Word**. This category covers designs that deconstruct the text. It's the smallest grouping but it's interesting that a number of designers have looked at word repetition and grammatical structure. We thought Robert Patten might find this approach disrespectful to the text, but he was intrigued by it, wondering whether there were algorithms applied and how these could reveal new levels of meaning in Dickens' language. These designs start to suggest how design can be a tool for analysis and research.

The next category is **Interaction**. The designs we have included under this heading foreground format and reading. Some look at how *Great Expectations* was originally published in serial form in *All The Year Round*, while in contrast, others explore how new platforms such as eReaders or quick response (QR) codes impact on reading. We've included designs in this category that are intentionally difficult to read in an attempt to increase appreciation and understanding. Several designers in this section referenced their own experience of reading, particularly as children, and how this informed their response to the brief. This grouping in particular includes designers who are interested in the activity of reading and its relationship to technology.

Image is a smaller group, and includes designs where the type is treated as image. These pieces are often figurative and generally more illustrative. While some designs in this section are playful and irreverent, others are more personal and evocative.

It was difficult to decide on a title for the section we eventually called **Tone**. We wondered about 'accent', but thought that too loaded. This category includes design systems that could be applied to the whole novel but where the typography is as much a graphic interpretation of the text as it is to be read. There are a number, for example, where changes in font size or similar visual disruptions are used to create an atmosphere of uncertainty or struggle. They're notable because the setting of fiction is usually more neutral, allowing the language to carry the meaning. These designs are some of the least conventional, and most awkward, in the book, primarily because this level of design intervention is rare in this context. They pose questions about what typography and layout can, and should, add to the experience of reading.

The final theme is **Story**. This includes designs that attempt to encapsulate the entire story in some way. They summarise themes, and as such act as illustrations of the whole book.

On the format

Our intention was always to publish *Page 1* as a conventional paperback book. Much has been written recently about emphasising the book as an object, and potentially a beautiful one at that. We wanted the format to be authentic – having asked the designers to lay out the first page of a novel, we wanted to publish the results in standard novel form. This was our version of the 'neutrality' mentioned previously, as it's a format that doesn't distract from the content. *Page 1* is for a design and non-design audience. It's not meant to signal that it's a design book. A paperback is affordable, it's democratic in that sense and of course there is still something lovely about an ordinary, standard paperback book.

It proved more difficult than we expected to find a proper book printer who would handle our relatively small print run and we ended up making rather a lot of obsessive phone calls about paper stock, grain direction and perfect binding that would allow the book to open relatively flat. Rather fortuitously we found our printers, Mackays, by looking at a recently printed paperback edition of *Great Expectations*.

On the one-volume novel

Contemporary readers experience Great Expectations *as a one-volume edition, which is the one form in which the book never originally appeared. This sets up certain expectations – they want it to be what a one-volume book is, ending in some kind of a resolution. I think the material instantiation is quite critical. I'd like to bring my students a book and a magazine and ask what they get out of holding the book, what their great expectation is when they pick up the book and then the magazine, because I think the materiality governs our response in so many ways.*

Of course if you were to publish Page 1 *in the original columns and format of* All The Year Round, *make your reader take their glasses off, and read in the dark by candle, this would be close to how* Great Expectations *was read originally. The columns would actually be easy to read because the light would fall directly on them – they wouldn't be lost in the shadows at the corners, and the effort to read by candlelight would pull you in, I suspect. Schematically, this would be very powerful.*

On the reader

We hope there'll be lots of different audiences interested in *Page 1*. It's hard not to sound idealistic when we say this but, in a small way, it makes the case for what design and designers can do. *Page 1* elucidates the influence that typography and design have on reading and although many of the responses are not viable typographic treatments for a new edition of *Great Expectations*, they do show a range of possibilities and the eagerness of designers to engage with the stories they give shape to. We've tried to make this book as accessible as possible, to designers and non-designers alike. By including the rationales and glossary our intention is to both inform and demystify the design process.

The book intentionally includes the work of a broad range of designers in terms of specialism, age, experience (some are current students), background and nationality and we're hugely grateful that so many accepted our invitation and for their generosity. After all, *Page 1* is not a compendium of work that already exists, but rather a collection of original pieces of work, which we hope our readers will enjoy looking at, whoever they may be.

On Dickens' likely reaction

Dickens could be very, very particular about the look of a page. If you were to look at Master Humphrey's Clock, an oddly formatted weekly periodical that set wood engravings into the text in ways that sometimes substituted the picture for the word, or at least expressed the same thought in both media collaboratively, you'd see evidence of Dickens' attention to the look of a page. And he could be a bear with compositors who misread his almost impossible-to-read penmanship. But at certain points in his life, more toward the end of his career when he turns to stage and then readings as primary means of reaching his audience, he seems to pay less attention to typography.

So, depending on his mood, he might say, 'Thanks for drawing my attention to this. I will go back to think about how Great Expectations might have affected readers differently in weekly columns and all-at-once three volumes. And I will talk with my printers about how my Charles Dickens Edition pages ought to look'. Or he might have said, 'It's the words, not the print, that matter, madam'.

The layout and printing

In print, red was the first colour to be employed alongside black, so these two colours are historically associated with typography. We have used both on the front cover, albeit in a contemporary way. It is printed in a fluorescent red and uses black foil-blocking, in part because its embossing is reminiscent of letterpress printing.

The fluorescent blocks on the cover represent the different folios from each *Page 1* design. Exceptions include solutions based on certain digital media, where page numbers do not apply.

Every contribution runs over four pages. The first spread shows the layout of the opening page of *Great Expectations*, the second carries the rationale.

Contributors are listed alphabetically within each theme.

The cover was printed on a Heidelberg Speedmaster sheet-fed press using Olin Rough Cream 300gsm board.

Widely used in paperback printing, the text stock is Ensonovel 70/140. The Timson web press used at CPI MacKays' Chatham plant is capable of printing 2,000 copies of a book in around ten minutes.

Each contributor's website address and individuals' year of birth and nationality are detailed on the second spread.

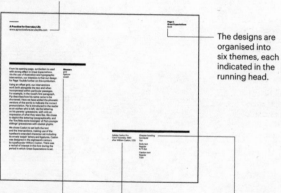

The designs are organised into six themes, each indicated in the running head.

There is a glossary of less common typographic terms at the end of the book. This is not exhaustive. It includes terms used more than once in the book that are not explained *in situ*. Included terms are listed next to any rationale in which they appear.

We asked contributors to supply information relating to the typefaces used in their layout. These details include typeface name/s, designer/s and date of issue or of design. The type foundry that either originally issued the font or currently supplies it is also listed.

Where designers have used a variety of weights and type sizes this information is also included.

A Practice for Everyday Life

CHAPTER 1

My father's family name being Pirrip ~pər-rɪp~, and my christian name Philip ~fɪ-lɪp~, my infant tongue could make of both names nothing longer or more explicit than Pip ~pɪp~. So, I called myself Pip, and came to be called Pip.

I give Pirrip as my father's family name, on the authority of his tombstone and my sister – Mrs. Joe Gargery, who married the blacksmith. As I never saw my father or my mother, and never saw any likeness of either of them (for their days were long before the days of photographs), my first fancies regarding what they were like, were unreasonably derived from their tombstones. The shape of the letters (fig. 1) on my father's, gave me an odd idea that he was a square, stout, dark man, with curly black hair. From the character and turn of the inscription, "Also Georgiana Wife of the Above," I drew a childish conclusion that my mother was freckled and sickly. To five little stone lozenges, each about a foot and a half long, which were arranged in a neat row beside their grave, and were sacred to the memory of five little brothers of mine – who gave up trying to get a living, exceedingly early in that universal struggle – I am indebted for a belief I religiously entertained that they had all been born on their backs with

FATHER

Mother

---

† † † † †

(fig. 1)

From its opening page, symbolism is used with strong effect in *Great Expectations*. Via the use of illustration and typographic intervention, our intention is that our design for *Page 1* builds further on this symbolism.

Using an offset grid, our interventions work both alongside the text and when incorporated within particular passages. For example, in the novel's first paragraph, Pip describes how his name came to be shortened. Here we have added the phonetic versions of the words to indicate the correct pronunciation. Pip is introduced to the reader as an orphan who is left, via the lettering on his parents' gravestone, with only an impression of what they were like. We chose to depict this lettering typographically, and the 'five little stone lozenges' of Pip's younger siblings' gravestones with obelisk glyphs.

We chose Caslon to set both the text and the interventions, making use of the typeface's extended character set including its ornate swash letters and ligatures. Caslon was designed in the eighteenth century by typefounder William Caslon. There was a revival of interest in this font during the period in which *Great Expectations* is set.

Glossary
grid
ligature
swash [character]

Adobe Caslon Pro
Carol Twombly, 1990
after William Caslon, 1725

Chapter heading
Semibold
11pt

Body text
Regular
9/11.3pt

Caption text
Regular
7.5pt

Phil Baines

I

My father's family name being Pirrip,
and my christian name Philip,
my infant tongue could make of both names nothing
longer or more explicit than Pip.
So, I called myself Pip,
and came to be called Pip.

I give Pirrip as my father's family name, on the authority of
his tombstone and my sister – Mrs Joe Gargery, who married the blacksmith. As I never saw my father or my mother,
and never saw any likeness of either of them (for their days
were long before the days of photographs), my first fancies
regarding what they were like, were unreasonably derived
from their tombstones. The shape of the letters on my father's, gave me an odd idea that he was a square, stout, dark
man, with curly black hair. From the character and turn of
the inscription, 'Also Georgiana Wife of the Above,' I drew
a childish conclusion that my mother was freckled and
sickly. To five little stone lozenges, each about a foot and a
half long, which were arranged in a neat row beside their
grave, and were sacred to the memory of five little brothers
of mine – who gave up trying to get a living, exceedingly
early in that universal struggle – I am indebted for a belief I
religiously entertained that they had all been born on their

Phil Baines
b1958/UK
www.flickr.com/photos/phil_baines/

Although I'm happy to work with short pieces of text (a sentence or two) and present them in a subjective manner for particular purposes, such an approach can be intrusive for longer passages. In the case of extracting and subjectively setting a single page from an entire novel, I liken it to watching a film with someone who insists on revealing the plot before each scene unfolds.

I wavered between setting a good-looking text page and taking an approach that was a little more subjective, something more celebratory of Dickens' bicentennial year. Having settled on the latter, I wanted to highlight and explore the origin of Pip's name, this had the advantage of keeping the typographic disruption at the very start of the page and served as an extended typographic introduction.

In broader terms, I found there was something unreal about designing a single page so I kept a complete spread in mind when laying out my design. The margins are more generous at the foot and fore-edge in order to create a harmonious spread, echoing the proportions of earlier printed books rather than a modern-day paperback.

Glossary
Modern [type]

The typeface is Bulmer, a British-taste
Modern typeface typical of the late
eighteenth century. Bulmer is not as wide
as Baskerville nor is it as 'spidery' as many
late nineteenth-century typefaces. The
text is set justified for easy linear reading.

Monotype Bulmer
Morris Fuller Benton for
American Type Founders, 1928
after William Martin c1790

Chapter number
Regular Small Caps
20pt

Display type
Regular
20pt

Body text
Regular
10.5/13pt

Folio
Regular Expert
10.5pt

Rupert Bassett

My father's family name being Pirrip, and my christian
name Philip, my infant tongue could make of both
names nothing longer or more explicit than Pip. So,
I called myself Pip, and came to be called Pip.

I give Pirrip as my father's family name, on the
authority of his tombstone and my sister — Mrs. Joe
Gargery, who married the blacksmith. As I never saw
my father or my mother, and never saw any likeness
of either of them (for their days were long before the
days of photographs), my first fancies regarding what
they were like, were unreasonably derived from their
tombstones. The shape of the letters on my father's,
gave me an odd idea that he was a square, stout, dark
man, with curly black hair. From the character and turn
of the inscription, 'Also Georgiana Wife of the Above,'
I drew a childish conclusion that my mother was
freckled and sickly. To five little stone lozenges, each
about a foot and a half long, which were arranged in
a neat row beside their grave, and were sacred to the
memory of five little brothers of mine — who gave up
trying to get a living, exceedingly early in that universal
struggle — I am indebted for a belief I religiously
entertained that they had all been born on their backs
with their hands in their trousers-pockets, and had
never taken them out in this state of existence.

Ours was the marsh country, down by the river,
within, as the river wound, twenty miles of the sea.
My first most vivid and broad impression of the identity
of things, seems to me to have been gained on a
memorable raw afternoon towards evening. At such
a time I found out for certain, that this bleak place
overgrown with nettles was the churchyard; and that
Philip Pirrip, late of this parish, and also Georgiana wife
of the above, were dead and buried; and that Alexander,
Bartholomew, Abraham, Tobias, and Roger, infant
children of the aforesaid, were also dead and buried;

Rupert Bassett
b1965/UK

For me, the essential appeal of the *Page 1* brief was that it gave an opportunity not just to challenge, but to totally dispense with the so-called 'classic' conventions of novel typesetting. In my design there are absolutely no visual references to the content; instead my intention was to create a simple and quietly efficient design system that could be applied to any text from any era.

The type specification is therefore unashamedly modernist. All the typographic elements are set asymmetrically, and are sized and positioned using a grid of uniform squares. Both the main body of text and navigational information at the head of the page are aligned left, while the page number is aligned right. My chosen typeface is Otl Aicher's Rotis Sans Serif 45 Light, set at a single type size of 10pt throughout.

Glossary
grid

Despite taking a modernist approach I used
imperial units of measurement instead of
metric. This converted the page dimensions
from a mathematically unhelpful 178 x 110mm
to a more user-friendly 42 x 26 picas.
This facilitated the systematic sizing and
positioning of all the elements using the
traditional typographic measurement
of picas as the base unit of the grid.
The line spacing interval is 1 pica or 12pts.
The paragraph indents are 2 picas. The
margins are sequentially 2 picas, 4 picas
and 6 picas. This creates a text area of
36 x 18 picas: an aesthetically and
intellectually satisfying double square.

Rotis Sans Serif 45 Light
Agfa
Otl Aicher, 1988
10/12pt

Book Works

CHAPTER ONE

Y FATHER'S FAMILY name being *Pirrip*, and my christian name *Philip*, my infant tongue could make of both names nothing longer or more explicit than *Pip*. So, I called myself *Pip*, and came to be called *Pip*. ❡ I give Pirrip as my father's family name, on the authority of his tombstone and my sister — Mrs. Joe Gargery, who married the blacksmith. As I never saw my father or my mother, and never saw any likeness of either of them (for their days were long before the days of photographs), my first fancies regarding what they were like, were unreasonably derived from their tombstones. The shape of the letters on my father's, gave me an odd idea that he was a **SQUARE, STOUT, DARK MAN, WITH CURLY BLACK HAIR.** From the character and turn of the inscription,"*Also Georgiana Wife of the Above,*" I drew a childish conclusion that my mother was freckled and sickly. To five little stone lozenges, each about a foot and a half long, which were arranged in a neat row beside their grave, and were sacred to the memory of five little brothers of mine — who gave up trying to get a living, exceedingly early in that universal struggle — I am indebted for a belief I religiously entertained that they had all been born on their backs with their hands in their trousers-pockets, and had never taken them out in this state of existence. ❡ Ours was the marsh country, down by the river, within, as the river wound, twenty miles of the sea. My first most vivid and broad impression of the identity of things, seems to me to have

Book Works
www.bookworks.org.uk

Claire Mason
b1973/UK

My *Page 1* design is a response to Dickens'
character-based narrative. This is reflected
in the choice of typeface and the typographic
detailing. The use of Sirenne with its
distinctive quirks and individual mannerisms
gives the body text character – even when
viewed as a block of text – and suggests the
personality of the narrator. This typeface
is derived from engraved letterforms used
in a rare natural history book from the early
eighteenth century. Developed to retain
the original quirks, Sirenne as a digitised
font has beautiful small caps, lively italics
and sturdy display versions – creating
a varied typographic palette with which
to add stress and character throughout the
text. Within this layout, my preference is
to add meaning through subtle typographic
variation. I have used some traditional
typographic conventions, such as setting
the opening paragraph in small caps, and
to indicate new paragraphs I have used
a paragraph symbol, creating a visual pause.
Lastly, I have played with the notion of
illustrated caps. I couldn't resist.

MVB Sirenne Text Roman TF
Alan Dague-Greene,
Mark van Bronkhorst, 2002

Body text
9.5/12pt

Folio
8.5pt

Chapter heading
MVB Sirenne Seventy-Two Small Caps
Roman
40pt

Tony Chambers

Chapter I

My father's family name being
Pirrip, and my christian name Philip,
my infant tongue could make of
both names nothing longer or more
explicit than Pip. So, I called
myself Pip, and came to be called

Pip.

I give Pirrip as my father's family
name, on the authority of his tombstone
and my sister – Mrs. Joe Gargery, who
married the blacksmith. As I never
saw my father or my mother, and never
saw any likeness of either of them
(for their days were long before the
days of photographs), my first fancies
regarding what they were like, were
unreasonably derived from their
tombstones. The shape of the letters
on my father's, gave me an odd idea
that he was a square, stout, dark
man, with curly black hair. From the
character and turn of the inscription,
'Also Georgiana Wife of the Above,'
I drew a childish conclusion that my
mother was freckled and sickly. To five
little stone lozenges, each about a foot
and a half long, which were arranged
in a neat row beside their grave, and
were sacred to the memory of five little
brothers of mine – who gave up trying
to get a living, exceedingly early in
that universal struggle – I am indebted
for a belief I religiously entertained that
they had all been born on their backs
with their hands in their trousers-pockets,
and had never taken them out in this
state of existence.

Ours was the marsh country, down
by the river, within, as the river wound,
twenty miles of the sea. My first most
vivid and broad impression of the
identity of things, seems to me to have

Tony Chambers
b1963/UK
www.wallpaper.com

Throughout my 25 years working in magazine publishing I've been obsessed with the avoidance of 'widows': a lonesome word at the end of a paragraph. Most experienced subeditors share this obsession, so very few have appeared in the pages I've watched over. But I can't deny that the odd one may have slipped through.

However, I can confidently claim that in the same period I have never been responsible for a typographic crime beyond comprehension, the appearance of an 'orphan' (a widow that falls at the top of a column). So, while ruminating on how to approach this lovely project, it dawned on me, with a perverse delight, that this was my chance to commit such a crime – and get away with it. Well, how else does one represent young Pip – who is surely the most famous literary orphan?

The chapter heading is set in Dala Floda designed by Paul Barnes and based upon the eroded lettering one might see on gravestones. I chose Baskerville to set the text. John Baskerville, born in 1706, was originally a letter cutter and writing master before he turned his hand to printing. It's highly likely that his days as a letter cutter would have involved the cutting of tombstones and the form of those letters may well have been the precursor to the font we now know as Baskerville. He may well have cut the letters that Pip describes in this passage.

Chapter heading
Dala Floda Medium
Commercial Type
Paul Barnes, 2010
16pt

Body text
Monotype Baskerville Regular
Monotype Type Drawing Office, 1923
after John Baskerville c1757
8/10pt

Folio
Monotype Baskerville Bold
Monotype Type Drawing Office, 1923
after John Baskerville c1757
7pt

Fred Birdsall studio

CHAPTER
I

My father's family name being Pirrip, and my christian name Philip, my infant tongue could make of both names nothing longer or more explicit than Pip. So, I called myself Pip, and came to be called Pip.

I give Pirrip as my father's family name, on the authority of his tombstone and my sister – Mrs. Joe Gargery, who married the blacksmith. As I never saw my father or my mother, and never saw any likeness of either of them (for their days were long before the days of photographs), my first fancies regarding what they were like, were unreasonably derived from their tombstones. The shape of the letters on my father's, gave me an odd idea that he was a square, stout, dark man, with curly black hair. From the character and turn of the inscription, *"Also Georgiana Wife of the Above,"* I drew a childish conclusion that my mother was freckled and sickly. To five little stone lozenges, each about a foot and a half long, which were arranged in a neat row beside their grave, and were sacred to the memory of five little brothers of mine – who gave up trying to get a living, exceedingly early in that universal struggle – I am indebted for a belief I religiously entertained that they had all been born on their backs with their hands in their trousers-pockets, and had never taken them out in this state of existence.

Ours was the marsh country, down by the river, within, as the river wound, twenty miles of the sea. My first most vivid and broad impression of the identity of things, seems

Fred Birdsall studio
www.birdsallstudio.org

Fred Birdsall
b1984/UK

I approached the *Page 1* brief as I would any other: as a 'proper' job. I initially focused on the choice of typeface. I felt that it should be English, preferably a serif and of the period of the novel. Trials were set in Caslon, Bulmer, Bell and Miller, after which I decided upon Bell, [1] partly because I find it extremely readable, but also because I find it rather handsome, especially the three-quarter height numerals (the first of their kind).

With regard to the layout, I constructed a straightforward, symmetrical grid. Chapter headings and folios are centered and running feet/headers are omitted. A justified setting (with hyphenation) was used for the text, which I find ideal for extended reading.

Glossary
grid
serif

[1]
Monotype Bell is
a facsimile of types cut
in London in 1788 by the
English punchcutter
Richard Austin
(1768–1830) for the
publisher John Bell
(1745–1831). It was
originally issued in
metal by Monotype in
1931 (the centenary of
John Bell's death).

Monotype Bell
Richard Austin, 1788

Chapter heading
Regular Small Capitals
14pt set solid

Body text, folio
Regular and Italic
10/13pt

Birna Geirfinnsdóttir

Chapter 1

My father's family name being Pirrip, and my christian
name Philip, my infant tongue could make of both
names nothing longer or more explicit than Pip. So,
I called myself Pip, and came to be called Pip.

I give Pirrip as my father's family name, on the
authority of his tombstone and my sister — Mrs. Joe
Gargery, who married the blacksmith. As I never saw
my father or my mother, and never saw any likeness
of either of them (for their days were long before the
days of photographs), my first fancies regarding what
they were like, were unreasonably derived from their
tombstones. The shape of the letters on my father's, gave
me an odd idea that he was a square, stout, dark man,
with curly black hair. From the character and turn of
the inscription, "Also Georgiana Wife of the Above," I drew
a childish conclusion that my mother was freckled and
sickly. To five little stone lozenges, each about a foot and
a half long, which were arranged in a neat row beside
their grave, and were sacred to the memory of five little
brothers of mine — who gave up trying to get a living,
exceedingly early in that universal struggle — I am
indebted for a belief I religiously entertained that they
had all been born on their backs with their hands in
their trousers-pockets, and had never taken them out in
this state of existence.

Ours was the marsh country, down by the river, within,
as the river wound, twenty miles of the sea. My first most
vivid and broad impression of the identity of things,
seems to me to have

Birna Geirfinnsdóttir
b1981/Iceland
www.birnageirfinns.com

I referenced books from my own personal
library that were printed in Iceland at the
same time as *Great Expectations* was issued
in Britain. I used these to inform my choice of
the relatively recently designed Miller, which
was influenced by early nineteenth-century
fonts. I also appropriated some of the
typographic detailing, where for instance
different type sizes are used instead of italic,
and reflected the crude letterpress printing
so the type alignments are sometimes
uneven and the type slightly distorted.
I think beauty can be found in these
imperfect details.

Miller Text
Font Bureau
Matthew Carter, 1997

Chapter heading
Bold
10pt

Body text
Roman
8.5pt and 10/12.75pt

Will Holder

One

MY FATHER'S FAMILY NAME being Pirrip, and my christian name Philip, my infant tongue could make of both names nothing longer or more explicit than Pip. So, I called myself Pip, and came to be called Pip.

I give Pirrip as my father's family name, on the authority of his tombstone and my sister – Mrs. Joe Gargery, who married the blacksmith. As I never saw my father or my mother, and never saw any likeness of either of them (for their days were long before the days of photographs), my first fancies regarding what they were like, were unreasonably derived from their tombstones. The shape of the letters on my father's, gave me an odd idea that he was a square, stout, dark man, with curly black hair. From the character and turn of the inscription, "Also Georgiana Wife of the Above," I drew a childish conclusion that my mother was freckled and sickly. To five little stone lozenges, each about a foot and a half long, which were arranged in a neat row beside their grave, and were sacred to the memory of five little brothers of mine – who gave up trying to get a living, exceedingly early in that universal struggle – I am indebted for a belief I religiously entertained that they had all been born on their backs with their hands in their trousers-pockets, and had never taken them out in this state of existence.

Ours was the marsh country, down by the river, within, as the river wound, twenty miles of the sea. My first most vivid and broad impression of the identity of things,

Will Holder
b1969/UK
www.commonknowledge.at

This page 1 finds its origins in the typesetting of *F.R.DAVID*, a journal which I edit and design – using the same stylesheets – since 2007. This convenience hopes to draw out some deviations made specifically with respect to Dickens' writing, over and above a discussion of choice of typeface, leading etc.

F.R.DAVID reproduces a selection of articles, with various authors and titles indicated at the top of each page (title left, author right) so that a reader may know where they are. With this novel's single title and author, a few hundred pages of 'Great Expectations', 'Charles Dickens', 'Great Expectations', 'Charles Dickens', 'Great Expectations', 'Charles Dickens' etc etc would seem like a distracting waste of ink.

Usually, the opening words of each article in *F.R.DAVID* would be typeset in small caps, where the amount of words selected would maintain a discrete unit of meaning. Set in this way, it would follow that the first 'Pirrip' in the first sentence would appear to be different, a visual irregularity – sadly distracting and diminishing Dickens' use of repetition with regard to the protagonist's absurd and unfortunate naming process. Further deviation is necessary for the sake of neatness: several kerned spaces have been inserted, in particular one between 'Mrs.' and 'Joe', so as not to break the proper noun 'Gargery'.

Glossary
drop capital

Lastly, since *F.R.DAVID* has an interest
in the self-reflexive production in
the space between names and things, or
the relation between writing and visual,
artistic production, it employs various
images as drop capitals. Dickens' opening
paragraphs, however, also allude to
the visual, even animistic characters of
typefaces, making the use of a visually
'freckled and sickly' font quite tempting.
However, I'd rather not draw attention away
from Dickens' original skill of using words
themselves to design images in the readers'
minds. Along with this, I understand that
this is an example of how a novel of a few
hundred pages might be typeset for reading,
and not a sample page to be looked at.

Typesetting specifics withheld

John Morgan studio

My father's family name being Pirrip, and my christian name Philip, my infant tongue could make of both names nothing longer or more explicit than Pip. So, I called myself Pip, and came to be called Pip.

I give Pirrip as my father's family name, on the authority of his tombstone and my sister – Mrs Joe Gargery, who married the blacksmith. As I never saw my father or my mother, and never saw any likeness of either of them (for their days were long before the days of photographs), my first fancies regarding what they were like, were unreasonably derived from their tombstones. The shape of the letters on my father's, gave me an odd idea that he was a square, stout, dark man, with curly black hair. From the character and turn of the inscription, *Also Georgiana Wife of the Above*, I drew a childish conclusion that my mother was freckled and sickly. To five little stone lozenges, each about a foot and a half long, which were arranged in a neat row beside their grave, and were sacred to the memory of five little brothers of mine – who gave up trying to get a living, exceedingly early in that universal struggle – I am indebted for a belief I religiously entertained that they had all been born on their backs with their hands in their trousers-pockets, and had never taken them out in this state of existence.

Ours was the marsh country, down by the river, within, as the river wound, twenty miles of the sea. My first most vivid and broad impression of the identity of things, seems to me to have been gained on a memorable raw afternoon towards evening. At such a time I found out for certain, that this bleak place overgrown

John Morgan studio
www.morganstudio.co.uk

John Morgan
b1973/UK

Another costume drama? No thanks.
No braces, no bonnets, no pastiche,
no parody, no irony. Why are there private
press charades in 'heritage Britain' that
reference the past and 'look forward'
to nostalgia? Should I raid the costume
department and open the cupboard –
try Caslon (fashionable again in 1860)
or Bulmer on for size? What about
a temporal resetting, as we might see
in theatre – Dickens in modern dress or
Pacino in Pucci?

What clothes should modern man wear?
I accept it, nothing really fits or feels
comfortable. Like Pip or good, honest-faced
Joe in a gentlemen's club, the typographer
could be stuck in a class-based identity
crisis. So I take the path of rightness and
lightness and choose Trinité by Bram de
Does, perhaps set a little bigger than
the reader may be used to, but then what
are they used to?

Word spaces made equal, as they should
be, no entrapment in a rigid Georgian
bed – it's ranged left and hyphenated,
self-determining within limits, just ragged
enough. I can resist a typographic gag –
to leave Pip as an orphan – instead, the
chapter number would sit alone on a blank
facing page. Although you see only a single
page here, my aim is to design for readers,
and after all these great expectations,
the final design does so little.

━━━━━━━━━━━━━━━━━━━━━━━━━━━━

And he is not likely to know what is to be done unless he lives in what is not merely the present, but the present moment of the past, unless he is conscious, not of what is dead, but of what is already living.

TS Eliot

━━━━━━━━━━━━━━━━━━━━━━━━━━━━

Trinité No 2 Roman Wide
Enschedé
Bram de Does, 1982
11.75/13.5pt

Robin Kinross

Chapter 1

My father's family name being Pirrip, and my christian name Philip, my infant tongue could make of both names nothing longer or more explicit than Pip. So, I called myself Pip, and came to be called Pip.

I give Pirrip as my father's family name, on the authority of his tombstone and my sister — Mrs. Joe Gargery, who married the blacksmith. As I never saw my father or my mother, and never saw any likeness of either of them (for their days were long before the days of photographs), my first fancies regarding what they were like, were unreasonably derived from their tombstones. The shape of the letters on my father's, gave me an odd idea that he was a square, stout, dark man, with curly black hair. From the character and turn of the inscription, 'Also Georgiana Wife of the Above', I drew a childish conclusion that my mother was freckled and sickly. To five little stone lozenges, each about a foot and a half long, which were arranged in a neat row beside their grave, and were sacred to the memory of five little brothers of mine — who gave up trying to get a living, exceedingly early in that universal struggle — I am indebted for a belief I religiously entertained that they had all been born on their backs with their hands in their trousers-pockets, and had never taken them out in this state of existence.

Ours was the marsh country, down by the river, within, as the river wound, twenty miles of the sea. My first most vivid and broad impression of the identity of things, seems to me to have been gained on a memorable raw afternoon towards evening. At such a time I found out for certain, that this bleak place overgrown with nettles was the churchyard; and that Philip Pirrip, late of this parish, and also Georgiana wife of the above, were dead and buried; and that Alexander, Bartholomew, Abraham, Tobias, and Roger, infant children of the aforesaid, were also

Robin Kinross
b1949/UK
www.hyphenpress.co.uk

I took the challenge to be one of finding a form for the whole novel, not just one page. So no special attention was given to these particular words: life is too short to do that over a long book. The deployment of space in the Collins edition referenced in the brief is extravagant: I needed to take more text. I wanted to make a page that could serve for any novel by Dickens – in fact for any novel written in the English language. The typeface used is fairly anonymous, but well made (Miller). Type size was found by trial and error, to get something that looked comfortable. I then worked with this capital height, adjusting it slightly to make it measure 2.2mm. This suggests a line increment (leading) double the capital height: 4.4mm. (See Peter Burnhill's analysis of Aldine typography in his book *Type Spaces*.) The 4.4mm unit was also chosen because it relates well to the 110mm page width (x 25). Margins, indents and positioning of chapter title and page number are determined by this module.

Glossary
leading

The inside margin is small (8.8mm) –
it presupposes a binding that lets the book
be fully opened and then stay flat. This
is possible with cold-glue or 'dispersion'
binding, which was the norm for perfect-
bound paperbacks in the UK into the 1970s;
it can still be found in Germany, Belgium,
the Netherlands and in the Far East.
Concerning the text: I cut the full point after
'Mrs', dropped the italic for the gravestone
inscription, and rearranged the punctuation
there – so that the comma stands outside
the quotation. The text is justified with a fairly
narrow average word space. Justified text
helps the sense of ordinariness and quietness
needed for this task.

Miller Text Roman
Font Bureau
Matthew Carter, 1997
9.1pt
baseline-to-baseline,
4.4mm

LucienneRoberts+

my father's family name being pirrip, and my
christian name philip, my infant tongue could
make of both names nothing longer or more
explicit than pip. so, i called myself pip, and came
to be called pip. —— i give pirrip as my father's
family name, on the authority of his tombstone
and my sister – mrs joe gargery, who married
the blacksmith. as i never saw my father or my
mother, and never saw any likeness of either of
them (for their days were long before the days
of photographs), my first fancies regarding what
they were like, were unreasonably derived from
their tombstones. the shape of the letters on
my father's, gave me an odd idea that he was
a square, stout, dark man, with curly black hair.
from the character and turn of the inscription,
'also georgiana wife of the above', i drew a
childish conclusion that my mother was freckled
and sickly. to five little stone lozenges, each about
a foot and a half long, which were arranged in
a neat row beside their grave, and were sacred
to the memory of five little brothers of mine –
who gave up trying to get a living, exceedingly
early in that universal struggle – i am indebted
for a belief i religiously entertained that they
had all been born on their backs with their hands
in their trousers-pockets, and had never taken
them out in this state of existence. —— ours was
the marsh country, down by the river, within, as
the river wound, twenty miles of the sea. my first
most vivid and broad impression of the identity
of things, seems to me to have been gained on

LucienneRoberts+
www.luciennerobertsplus.com

Lucienne Roberts
b1962/UK

I never really 'got' typography as
a student, until being set the simple but
oh-so-enlightening brief to design an
invitation in one font using only space
or one change in type weight or type size
or one other colour alongside black for
emphasis. It was one of those Damascene
moments! I quickly came to understand the
potential of each variant and wholeheartedly
embraced the maxim 'less is more'.

Not long after graduation, I worked part-
time as an in-house designer at a feminist
publisher of both fiction and non-fiction
books. These were groundbreaking,
provocative and often irreverent, so I was
baffled by the conventional layout of
the text – centred (of course), serif type
(of course), indents and so on. I considered
the pages an anachronism, at odds with
the books' modern covers.

I still stand by this in terms of consistency
and appropriateness but I have come to
understand that taking things away isn't
always so minimal – or sympathetic to
the text. Some design conventions are so
prevalent as to be almost invisible, so
changing them is high design intervention
rather than the opposite. That said, I simply
can't centre anything – it seems so illogical
as we read from left to right – and a slab serif
is about as far as I can go down that road.

Glossary
sans serif

All this acts as background to my layout for *Page 1*. Taking that student exercise as a starting point, it uses one sans serif font in one type size and one weight. I was interested to test how far this 'minimalism' could go and so all the capitals have been removed too. I would generally use half line spaces between paragraphs but as I don't like to split them over pages have run the text on, with rules rather like long dashes to signal a paragraph break. The baseline grid is a ridiculous 1.5pt (3pt being my favourite). The text is ranged left and positioned asymmetrically on the page. The left hand margin is 15mm and the text runs over a 65mm measure (two 30mm columns plus a 5mm inter-column space). In keeping with the approach to typography and layout, I have used single quotes, omitted the full point after 'mrs' and transposed the comma and closing quote of the inscription.

So, in my terms this is a minimal approach but in terms of how it overshadows the text I suspect it's sadly the opposite...

Akzidenz-Grotesk BQ Light OsF
Berthold
Hermann Berthold, 1898
typeface family enlarged by
Günter Gerhard Lange, 1950s
9/10.5pt

Catherine Nippe

CHAPTER 1

My father's family name being Pirrip, and my christian name Philip, my infant tongue could make of both names nothing longer or more explicit than Pip. So, I called myself Pip, and came to be called Pip.

I give Pirrip as my father's family name, on the authority of his tombstone and my sister – Mrs. Joe Gargery, who married the blacksmith. As I never saw my father or my mother, and never saw any likeness of either of them (for their days were long before the days of photographs), my first fancies regarding what they were like, were unreasonably derived from their tombstones. The shape of the letters on my father's, gave me an odd idea that he was a square, stout, dark man, with curly black hair. From the character and turn of the inscription, *"Also Georgiana Wife of the Above,"* I drew a childish conclusion that my mother was freckled and sickly. To five little stone lozenges, each about a foot and a half long, which were arranged in a neat row beside their grave, and were sacred to the memory of five little brothers of mine – who gave up trying to get a living, exceedingly early in that universal struggle – I am indebted for a belief I religiously entertained that they had all been born on their backs with their hands in their trousers-pockets, and had never taken them out in this state of existence.

Ours was the marsh country, down by the river, within, as the river wound, twenty miles of the sea. My first most vivid and broad impression of the identity of

Catherine Nippe
b1978/Switzerland/Germany
www.cnippe.com

The first page of any novel is significant;
it literally holds great expectation. It forms
the opening of the narrative as well as
defining the beginning of the physical object
of the book. In most Latin books the first
page is a recto (right-hand page), which is
read by turning the pages from right to left,
propelling a reader forward into the book
and never backwards. As a reader we meet
the first page with anticipation and curiosity
as to what will follow – it constitutes the
beginning of a journey.

My *Page 1* design reflects and accentuates
the recto page. The outside margins
are wider than the inside. These refer
to traditional book proportions and the
golden section. However, my top and
bottom margins are not determined by
these principles. They are more modern
in allowing more copy to fit on the page
than would have been the case had
I applied the golden ratio throughout.

The page number and chapter headings
don't align with the margins, creating
additional stress and placing more emphasis
on the asymmetric page layout. Type size
is rather small and the leading is tight
in order to hold approximately 2,000
characters per page, and make this
a compact book despite the overall word
count. Arnhem Blond was used for its
modern, legible qualities and the edge
I think it brings.

Arnhem Blond
OurType
Fred Smeijers, 2002

Chapter heading, folio
7.5pt

Body text
9.25/11pt

Ian Noble

CHAPTER ONE

My FATHER's family name being Pirrip, and my
christian name Philip, my infant tongue could
make of both names nothing longer or more
explicit than Pip. So, I called myself Pip, and
came to be called Pip. I give Pirrip as my FATHER's
family name, on the authority of his tombstone
and my SISTER — Mrs. Joe Gargery, who married the
blacksmith. As I never saw my FATHER or my MOTHER,
and never saw any likeness of either of them (for
their days were long before the days of photographs),
my first fancies regarding what they were like, were
unreasonably derived from their tombstones.
The shape of the letters on my FATHER's, gave me an
odd idea that he was a square, stout, dark man, with
curly black hair. From the character and turn of the
inscription, "Also Georgiana WIFE of the Above,"
I drew a childish conclusion that my MOTHER was
freckled and sickly. To five little stone lozenges,
each about a foot and a half long, which were
arranged in a neat row beside their grave, and were
sacred to the memory of five little BROTHERS of
mine — who gave up trying to get a living, exceedingly
early in that universal struggle — I am indebted for a
belief I religiously entertained that they had all been
born on their backs with their hands in their trousers-
pockets, and had never taken them out in this state
of existence. Ours was the marsh country, down by
the river, within, as the river wound, twenty miles of
the sea. My first most vivid and broad impression of
the identity of things, seems to me to have

Ian Noble
b1960/UK

I have enjoyed *Great Expectations*, both as a film and a novel, throughout my life. When I was younger, my strongest memory of the story was David Lean's film version and the figure of Magwitch, played by the actor Finlay Currie (the film also starred John Mills and Alec Guinness). I have a clear recollection of the fear created, not by the physical appearance of Magwitch, but because of my own identification with Pip and his vulnerability as a small child terrorised by an escaped adult prisoner on the run. Robert De Niro reprised this role in the 1998 version of the film and whilst I wasn't as scared by this performance (I was older and, to a greater extent I hope, less impressionable), I was again reminded of how I had felt when younger.

My watching and reading became my own version of a 'rights of passage' or *Bildungsroman* tale. In between watching these two versions of the film I read the novel, both under instruction at school and then later recreationally, and it occupies a particular place in my memory. I think the story in all its iterations is about class, power and relationships and, in particular, about what we think we know to be true.

Glossary
diphthong
ligature

I tried to think about how I could design the page so that the text could be easily read and how, through the addition of graphic devices and choice of typeface and tone, a second level of information could be delivered (albeit in a subtle fashion).

I have used Mrs Eaves, which was drawn by Zuzana Licko in 1996 for Emigre fonts. It is named after Sarah Eaves, who married John Baskerville and continued their work after his death, but who is rarely mentioned in typographic histories (itself like a Dickensian plot). I also chose this font because of its fantastic diphthongs, ligatures and small caps, all of which I have used to emphasise relationships and connections.

The novel's first page is full of references to parents and family; a theme that runs throughout the book. The tonal variation is used to reveal further the structure of the novel and Pip's two roles as central character and narrator.

Mrs Eaves
Roman, Petite Caps, Small Caps
and Just Ligatures
Emigre
Zuzana Licko, 1996
11/13pt

Pentagram

y father's family name being Pirrip, and my christian name Philip, my infant tongue could make of both names nothing longer or more explicit than Pip. So, I called myself Pip, and came to be called Pip.

I give Pirrip as my father's family name, on the authority of his tombstone and my sister – Mrs. Joe Gargery, who married the blacksmith. As I never saw my father or my mother, and never saw any likeness of either of them (for their days were long before the days of photographs), my first fancies regarding what they were like, were unreasonably derived from their tombstones. The shape of the letters on my father's, gave me an odd idea that he was a square, stout, dark man, with curly black hair. From the character and turn of the inscription, "Also Georgiana Wife of the Above," I drew a childish conclusion that my mother was freckled and sickly. To five little stone lozenges, each about a foot and a half long, which were arranged in a neat row beside their grave, and were sacred to the memory of five little brothers of mine – who gave up trying to get a living, exceedingly early in that universal struggle – I am indebted for a belief I religiously entertained that they had all been born on their backs with their hands in their trousers-pockets, and had never taken

Pentagram
www.pentagram.com

Luke Hayman
b1966/UK

My idea here was a simple one: to create a contemporary version of an illustrated drop cap. These mostly decorative elements can set the tone for a book and provide an identity.

I decided to explore photography, which is a modern illustration method. However, one potential problem with photography and fiction is that it can be too specific; it's important that the reader is able to form their own images of characters and place (the reason to read the book before you see the film). My solution was to heavily blur Pip's image – there's enough information to imply a young English boy's face, but not enough to impose a personality or imply a specific person.

Glossary
drop capital

Arnhem Blond
OurType
Fred Smeijers, 2002
9.25/11pt

Ray Roberts

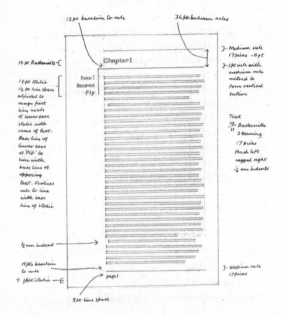

12pt baseline to rule

36pts between rules

14-pt Baskerville

14-pt Italic
½ pc line space
adjusted to
range first
line heads
of lower case
italic with
same of text.
Base line of
lower case
of 'Pip' to
line with
base line of
opposing
text. Vertical
rule to line
with base
line of italic

Chapter 1

how I
became
Pip

Medium rule
17 picas + 5 pt

1 pt rule with
medium rule
mitred to
form vertical
section

Text
10 Baskerville
11 o kerning
17 picas
flush left
ragged right
½ em indents

½ em indent

15 pts baseline
to rule

9 ½ pt italic

page 1

Medium rule
17 picas

5 pt line space

Chapter 1

*how I
became
Pip*

My father's family name being Pirrip, and
my christian name Philip, my infant tongue
could make of both names nothing longer
or more explicit than Pip. So, I called myself
Pip, and came to be called Pip.

I give Pirrip as my father's family name, on
the authority of his tombstone and my sister –
Mrs Joe Gargery, who married the blacksmith.
As I never saw my father or my mother,
and never saw any likeness of either of them
(for their days were long before the days of
photographs), my first fancies regarding what
they were like, were unreasonably derived
from their tombstones. The shape of the letters
on my father's, gave me an odd idea that he
was a square, stout, dark man, with curly
black hair. From the character and turn of the
inscription, *'Also Georgiana Wife of the Above'*,
I drew a childish conclusion that my mother
was freckled and sickly. To five little stone
lozenges, each about a foot and a half long,
which were arranged in a neat row beside their
grave, and were sacred to the memory of five
little brothers of mine who gave up trying
to get a living, exceedingly early in that
universal struggle – I am indebted for a belief
I religiously entertained that they had all been
born on their backs with their hands in their
trousers-pockets, and had never taken them
out in this state of existence.

Ours was the marsh country, down by the
river, within, as the river wound, twenty miles
of the sea. My first most vivid and broad
impression of the identity of things, seems to

Ray Roberts
b1925/UK

The architecture of a book is usually based on the design of a double-page opening. The *Page 1* task does not mention this point and it must therefore be assumed that solutions could be approached quite literally as a single page.

However, I have followed normal practice by designing a layout as the first page of a sequence of pages. For example, on subsequent pages the uppermost rule would become an underline to small italic running headlines relating to the narrative. In the often-complex texts of Victorian novels, such headlines were considered to be helpful in referencing content. In similar fashion, books of the time also used short summaries of content at chapter openings; hence my suggested use of short introductions on the first page of a chapter (these could be up to six lines in depth).

Apart from these small archaisms the treatment of the layout is fairly straightforward and simple. Baskerville has been selected because, historically, it is among those Roman type forms that retained bracketed serifs before the advent of the Moderns. By the mid-nineteenth century these latter forms had become overly thin.

Glossary
Modern [type]
Roman [type]
serif

I have made a few small amendments to the text as supplied – deleting the full point after Mrs, using single quotation marks and transposing the closing quote mark and comma after the inscription. This is more in keeping with my contemporary approach to both the layout and typographic detailing of the text.

Standard practice in the period that I worked was to give a marked-up layout to the typesetter. This is shown on page 086. As would often be the case, minor adjustments have been made to the final design.

Monotype Baskerville
Monotype Type Drawing Office, 1923
after John Baskerville c1757

Chapter heading
Regular
14pt

Display
Italic
14pt

Body text
Regular and Italic
10/11pt

Folio
Italic
10pt

Judith Schalansky

CHAPTER I

My father's family name being Pirrip, and my chriſtian name Philip, my infant tongue could make of both names nothing longer or more explicit than Pip. So, I called myſelf Pip, and came to be called Pip.

I give Pirrip as my father's family name, on the authority of his tombſtone and my ſiſter—Mrs. Joe Gargery, who married the blackſmith. As I never ſaw my father or my mother, and never ſaw any likeneſs of either of them (for their days were long before the days of photographs), my firſt fancies regarding what they were like, were unreaſonably derived from their tombſtones. The ſhape of the letters on my father's, gave me an odd idea that he was a ſquare, ſtout, dark man, with curly black hair. From the character and turn of the inſcription, "*Alſo Georgiana Wife of the Above,*" I drew a childiſh concluſion that my mother was freckled and ſickly. To five little ſtone lozenges, each about a foot and a half long, which were arranged in a neat row beſide their grave, and were ſacred to the memory of five little brothers of mine—who gave up try-ing to get a living, exceedingly early in that univerſal ſtruggle— I am indebted for a belief I religiouſly entertained that they had all been born on their backs with their hands in their trouſers-pockets, and had never taken them out in this ſtate of exiſtence.

Ours was the marſh country, down by the river, within, as the river wound, twenty miles of the ſea. My firſt moſt vivid and broad impreſſion of the identity of things, ſeems to me to have

Judith Schalansky
b 1980/Germany
www.judith-schalansky.de

An English novel, set in a French Renaissance Antiqua, designed by a German type designer.

I've selected Fabiol, designed by Robert Strauch and available from Lazydogs Typefoundry, for my *Page 1* design. Fabiol not only offers strong contours, but also an odd and almost forgotten detail of type history: the long 's', which was commonly used until the middle of the nineteenth century and which I have used selectively here. Today it could be seen as a small but distinguished detail to remind us of Pip's achievement in becoming a gentleman.

Glossary
French Renaissance Antiqua [text]

Fabiol
Regular, Italic and Caps
Lazydogs Typefoundry
Robert Strauch, 2006
10.2/14.5pt

Erik Spiekermann

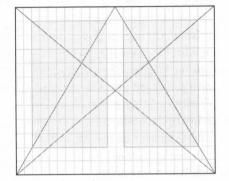

who gave up tryin
universal struggle
entertained that t
their hands in the
them out in this st
    Ours was th
as the river woun
vivid and broad im
me to have been

of mine – who gave
in that universal s
giously entertaine
backs with their l
never taken them
    Ours was
within, as the rive
most vivid and br
seems to me to l

MY FATHER'S FAMILY name being Pirrip, and my christian name Philip, my infant tongue could make of both names nothing longer or more explicit than Pip. So, I called myself Pip, and came to be called Pip.

I give Pirrip as my father's family name, on the authority of his tombstone and my sister – Mrs. Joe Gargery, who married the blacksmith. As I never saw my father or my mother, and never saw any likeness of either of them (for their days were long before the days of photographs), my first fancies regarding what they were like, were unreasonably derived from their tombstones. The shape of the letters on my father's, gave me an odd idea that he was a square, stout, dark man, with curly black hair. From the character and turn of the inscription, *"Also Georgiana Wife of the Above,"* I drew a childish conclusion that my mother was freckled and sickly. To five little stone lozenges, each about a foot and a half long, which were arranged in a neat row beside their grave, and were sacred to the memory of five little brothers of mine – who gave up trying to get a living, exceedingly early in that universal struggle – I am indebted for a belief I religiously entertained that they had all been born on their backs with their hands in their trousers-pockets, and had never taken them out in this state of existence.

Ours was the marsh country, down by the river, within, as the river wound, twenty miles of the sea. My first most vivid and broad impression of the identity of things, seems to me to have been gained on a memorable raw after-

Erik Spiekermann
b1947/Germany
www.edenspiekermann.com

The page dimensions supplied in the *Page 1*
brief are exactly 1:1.618; the proportions
of the golden section. I took this as a hint
and went for the simplest construction
by dividing the page into 12 units in both
directions. Each of the resulting page units
has the same proportions as the whole
page; not important for a book without
illustrations, but useful for working out
the margins: two units bottom and outside,
one unit each for inside and top. The folio
falls outside the type area and is indented by
half the amount of the text indents, lest it
appear to stand out too far to the right or left.

I found the choice of type difficult. I keep
finding great new interpretations of classic
text faces and often buy them spontaneously,
as I did with Genath, shown bottom left on
page 094. Designed by François Rappo in
Lausanne, Genath is based on the work of
Johann Wilhelm Haas for the Genath foundry
in Basel. I welcomed such a golden [sic]
opportunity to use François' interpretation
of a baroque type. It seemed appropriate
because Dickens' books were probably set in
one of Caslon's types, originally designed
in the eighteenth century and brought back
into production around 1844, during the
Neo-Renaissance movement in Britain.

Glossary
folio
sans serif

But then I reconsidered. If this were to be one of a general series of books with classic texts, I might go for the version set in Lyon, shown bottom right on page 094 and designed by Kai Bernau. It follows the Robert Granjon/Garamond model and is a contemporary magazine face as used by the *New York Times Magazine*. A little slick perhaps, but the potential readers may not have been brought up on the classics.

Finally, however, vanity demanded that I use one of my faces. This one is Unit Slab, not a book face but one that makes the text look contemporary. Traditional publishers wouldn't have it, but if it makes Dickens look more modern, it might get new readers to actually engage.

My layout is very conservative. The text is justified, with around 55 characters per line to avoid terrible hyphenation, and I think that 10/13.2pt type is what readers expect in a book this size. The paragraph indents of 10mm are a little more generous than the classic em because I like a proper pause in a long text. The chapter heading is set in Akzidenz Grotesk Super, also first designed in the nineteenth century and reminiscent of Caslon's first sans serif. A little contrast seemed in order, so I also set the folio in that face, at 7pt like the heading. I used no tricks, just normal typesetting parameters. All the following pages would look just like this one.

Chapter heading, folio
Akzidenz Grotesk Super
Berthold
Günter Gerhard Lange, 1968

Body text
FF Unit Slab Pro
Regular, Italic and
Medium Small Caps
FontFont
Christian Schwartz,
Erik Spiekermann,
Kris Sowersby, 2009
10/13.2pt

Studio Andrew Howard

CHAPTER I

My father's family name being Pirrip, and my christian name Philip, my infant tongue could make of both names nothing longer or more explicit than Pip. So, I called myself Pip, and came to be called Pip.

I give Pirrip as my father's family name, on the authority of his tombstone and my sister – Mrs. Joe Gargery, who married the blacksmith. As I never saw my father or my mother, and never saw any likeness of either of them (for their days were long before the days of photographs), my first fancies regarding what they were like, were unreasonably derived from their tombstones. The shape of the letters on my father's, gave me an odd idea that he was a square, stout, dark man, with curly black hair. From the character and turn of the inscription, *"Also Georgiana Wife of the Above"*, I drew a childish conclusion that my mother was freckled and sickly.

Studio Andrew Howard
www.studioandrewhoward.com

Andrew Howard
b1956/UK

In the past I've been sympathetic to the argument that images in literary works diminish the reader's potential to create their own mental pictures – the ability to imagine for oneself. And yet I'm also drawn to their potential to stir the imagination. I remember as a boy being captivated by the world that some illustrated books were able to draw me into. So, despite initially exploring ideas for purely typographic layouts, I opted to include images (I saw this as the first of many pages), with the idea of establishing a mood and setting through illustration and typographic styles combined.

The small format of the book was influential in this desire, and a larger format would probably have led me elsewhere. In his work Dickens creates a story rich in intricate detail and human sentiment, a world I wanted to echo in the aesthetic of the design.

Portraying the village church and cemetery, the illustration (from a clip art site), although not as menacing as the graveyard scene to follow, has other qualities; the fine detail of the drawing, its unboxed contours, and the 'Englishness' of the scene it depicts. The title face is Gotham from Hoefler & Frere-Jones. The text face is Parry by Artur Schmal and is set 8.5/13.5pt. This is set in a deliberately small point size in which the detail of the slab serif, together with the detail of the drawing, combine to create the humanity and richness I wish to reflect.

Chapter heading
Gotham Bold
Hoefler & Frere-Jones
Tobias Frere-Jones, 2000

Text, folio
Parry Normal
OurType
Artur Schmal, 2006
8.5/13.5pt

Studio EMMI

My father's family name being Pirrip, and my christian name
Philip, my infant tongue could make of both names nothing longer
or more explicit than Pip. So, I called myself Pip, and came to be
called Pip.

I give Pirrip as my father's family name, on the authority of his
tombstone and my sister – Mrs. Joe Gargery, who married the
blacksmith. As I never saw my father or my mother, and never saw
any likeness of either of them (for their days were long before the
days of photographs), my first fancies regarding what they were
like, were unreasonably derived from their tombstones. The shape
of the letters on my father's, gave me an odd idea that he was a
square, stout, dark man, with curly black hair. From the character
and turn of the inscription, *"Also Georgiana Wife of the Above,"*
I drew a childish conclusion that my mother was freckled and
sickly. To five little stone lozenges, each about a foot and a half
long, which were arranged in a neat row beside their grave, and
were sacred to the memory of five little brothers of mine – who
gave up trying to get a living, exceedingly early in that universal
struggle – I am indebted for a belief I religiously entertained that
they had all been born on their backs with their hands in their
trousers-pockets, and had never taken them out in this state
of existence.

Ours was the marsh country, down by the river, within, as the
river wound, twenty miles of the sea. My first most vivid and
broad impression of the identity of things, seems to me to have

Studio EMMI
www.emmi.co.uk

Emmi Salonen
b1977/Finland

I chose to approach my *Page 1* design as if I were planning to lay out the entire novel. No fancy type treatments, just easily legible layout so the reader can concentrate on the content. I chose to use Vista Sans Alt Regular for the body copy and Bold for the chapter numbers and folios.

Glossary
folio

Vista Sans Alt
Emigre
Xavier Dupré, 2005

Chapter heading, folio
Bold
6.5pt

Body text
Regular
7.5/11pt

Mark Thomson

Chapter 1

My father's family name being Pirrip, and my christian name
Philip, my infant tongue could make of both names nothing
longer or more explicit than Pip. So, I called myself Pip, and
came to be called Pip.

I give Pirrip as my father's family name, on the authority of
his tombstone and my sister – Mrs Joe Gargery, who married the
blacksmith. As I never saw my father or my mother, and never
saw any likeness of either of them (for their days were long before
the days of photographs), my first fancies regarding what they
were like, were unreasonably derived from their tombstones.
The shape of the letters on my father's, gave me an odd idea that
he was a square, stout, dark man, with curly black hair. From
the character and turn of the inscription, '*Also Georgiana Wife
of the Above*', I drew a childish conclusion that my mother was
freckled and sickly. To five little stone lozenges, each about a
foot and a half long, which were arranged in a neat row beside
their grave, and were sacred to the memory of five little brothers
of mine – who gave up trying to get a living, exceedingly early in
that universal struggle – I am indebted for a belief I religiously
entertained that they had all been born on their backs with their
hands in their trousers-pockets, and had never taken them out
in this state of existence.

Ours was the marsh country, down by the river, within, as
the river wound, twenty miles of the sea. My first most vivid and
broad impression of the identity of things, seems to me to have

1

Mark Thomson
b1961/UK
www.markthomsondesign.com

This sample has been typeset using
a system in which word spacing varies
contextually around a median value,
giving a semi-justified text block.

A median word space value is defined
and parameters are set equally above and
below this value. In this example the median
value is 90% and the variation is plus or
minus 10%. The method is applied to each
line with reference to the preceding and
following lines, in such a way that word
spacing does not vary by more than 10%
from one line to the next, ie a line of 100%
word spaces cannot be followed by one
of 80%.

Line endings can be determined by the
requirements of the text, as in unjustified
setting, and by the quality of undulation
in the right edge. Exceptionally, individual
lines may extend outside the text frame;
the number and degree of exceptions can
be defined. In this sample, the fourth line of
the second paragraph extends about 1mm
outside the frame.

The result is a semi-justified text block with
relatively even word spacing and a tighter
right edge than conventional unjustified
text. The modern British punctuation style
of single quotes is used.

Arnhem Pro Blond
OurType
Fred Smeijers, 2002–10
8.5/11pt

Typographics

Chapter one

I give Pirrip as my father's family name, on the authority of his tombstone and my sister Mrs Joe Gargery, who married the blacksmith.

My father's family name being Pirrip, and my christian name Philip, my infant tongue could make of both names nothing longer or more explicit than Pip. So, I called myself Pip, and came to be called Pip.

As I never saw my father or my mother, and never saw any likeness of either of them *for their days were long before the days of photographs*, my first fancies regarding what they were like, were unreasonably derived from their tombstones.

The shape of the letters on my father's, gave me an odd idea that he was a square, stout, dark man, with curly black hair. From the character and turn of the inscription, *Also Georgiana Wife of the Above*, I drew a childish conclusion that my mother was freckled and sickly. To five little stone lozenges, each about a foot and a half long, which were arranged in a neat row beside their grave, and were sacred to the memory of five little brothers of mine *who gave up trying to get a living, exceedingly early in that universal struggle* I am indebted for a belief I religiously entertained that they had all been born on their backs with their hands in their trousers-pockets, and had never taken them out in this state of existence.

Ours was the marsh country, down by the river, within, as the river wound, twenty miles of the sea. My

Typographics
www.typographics.co.uk

Eugenie Dodd
b 'I knew Anthony Froshaug'/UK/Israel

To me, *Page 1* is less about typography and more about a book 'experience'. *Great Expectations* is written in an energetic prose style incorporating vivid sketches, unpredictable connections and shifts of tone. Dickens' rural and urban landscapes are graphically described with a strong sense of atmosphere and place. This is a seductive canvas for the use of typography as an additional expressive layer.

I consider my solution to be a form of visual prose – a kind of annotation of the text and a way of commenting on the original story. I have identified different modes of writing within this narrative, which I have signalled using layout and typography. My typographic styling derives from techniques used by jobbing printers since the nineteenth century, many of which are still used today for advertising and display typography.

My design has two aims: to raise the reader's awareness of the visual qualities of textual narration, and to set up a system for others to follow in setting the book beyond its first page.

Glossary
sans serif
serif

The parameters I have set are:

- angled text columns (based on grid points 5mm apart) to create dynamic rhythm and space
- serif and sans serif typefaces in a broad range of weights for emphasis
- ranged left and ranged right typesetting to give texture and movement
- paragraph indents that follow previous line endings to add momentum

Photina MT Std
Monotype
José Mendoza y Almeida, 1971
Semibold 9.5/11pt
Semibold Italic 9.5/12.5pt

Bliss
JT Types Ltd
Jeremy Tankard, 1996
Regular 13pt set solid
Extra bold 13/17pt
Light 9/13pt

Rebecca Wright

chapter one

my father's family name being pirrip,
and my christian name philip, my infant
tongue could make of both names
nothing longer or more explicit than pip.
so, i called myself pip, and came to be
called pip.

i give pirrip as my father's family name,
on the authority of his tombstone and
my sister – mrs joe gargery, who married
the blacksmith. as i never saw my father
or my mother, and never saw any likeness
of either of them (for their days were
long before the days of photographs),
my first fancies regarding what they
were like, were unreasonably derived
from their tombstones.

the shape of the letters on my father's,
gave me an odd idea that he was a square,
stout, dark man, with curly black hair.

Rebecca Wright
b1972/UK

Professor Robert Patten comments at the beginning of this book that we should remember the original readers of *Great Expectations* would have likely read by candlelight, and that the two-column layout of *All The Year Round*, in which it was first published, would have been helpful in this regard.

This *Page 1* design is set in Tiresias LPfont, [1] a large print typeface designed for people with low vision by Dr John Gill of the Scientific Research Unit at the Royal National Institute for Blind People (RNIB). The Tiresias LPfont family is specifically for use in large print publications and comprises Roman, Italic and Bold weights, with particular focus on the contrasting shape and weight of characters and details such as letter and word spacing.

Working within the confines of the format, the text has been set to adhere to both the RNIB Clear Print guidelines [2] and the *Dyslexia Style Guide*, [3] published by the British Dyslexia Society.

In line with Clear Print guidelines, the type is 12/18pt, the use of capital letters has been avoided, the chapter heading is distinguished through type weight rather than style, the elements on the page are clearly separated with space between each paragraph and the text is ranged left. In addition, the text follows the *Dyslexia Style Guide* recommendation that new sentences do not start at the end of a line, and long paragraphs have been divided into smaller ones.

This *Page 1* design uses a free download font and is set according to publicly available guidelines. The aim is for the design to be easily legible for the widest audience and to be easily replicable, objectives I think Charles Dickens might just have approved of.

[1]
www.tiresias.org/fonts

[2]
Clear Print guidelines,
RNIB, www.rnib.org.uk

[3]
Dyslexia Style Guide
British Dyslexia
Association
www.bdadyslexia.org.uk

Tiresias LPfont
Dr John Gill for the Royal National
Institute for Blind People (RNIB)
Based on Tiresias, 1998

Chapter heading
Tiresias LPfont Bold
14/18pt

Body text
Tiresias LPfont Roman
12/18pt

Barnbrook

Chapter 1

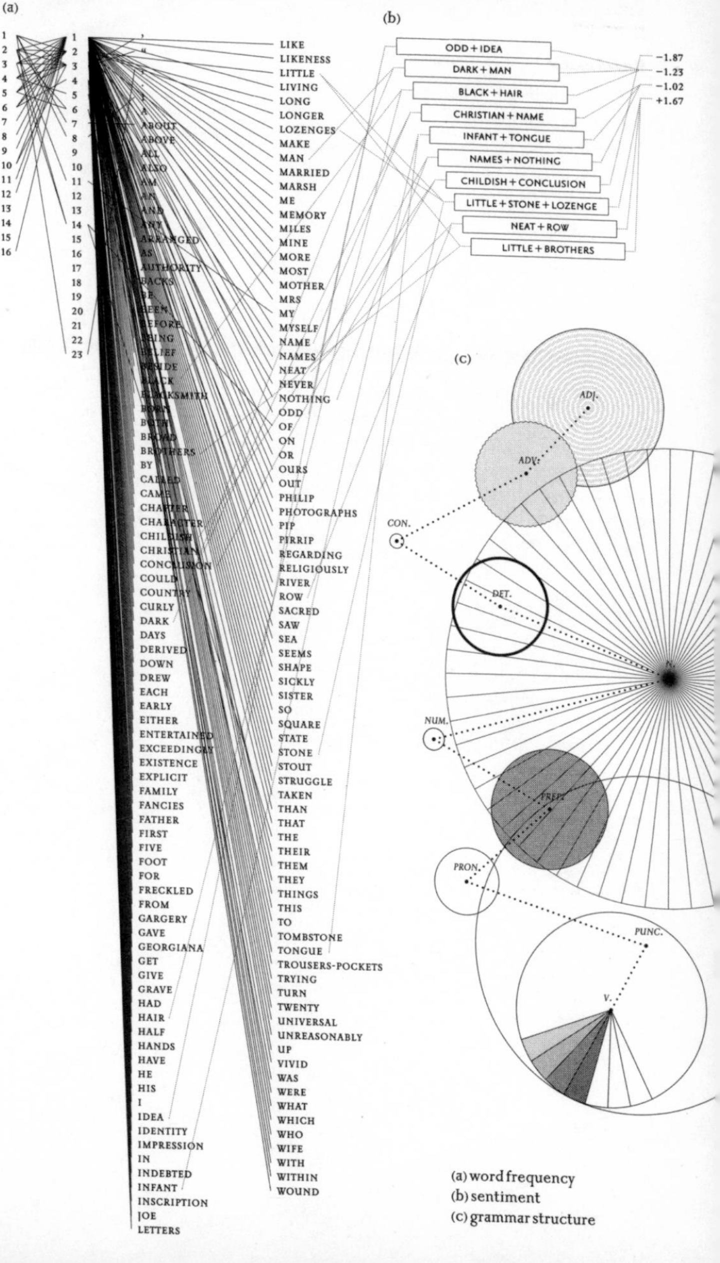

(a)

(b)

(c)

ODD + IDEA	−1.87
DARK + MAN	−1.23
BLACK + HAIR	−1.02
CHRISTIAN + NAME	+1.67
INFANT + TONGUE	
NAMES + NOTHING	
CHILDISH + CONCLUSION	
LITTLE + STONE + LOZENGE	
NEAT + ROW	
LITTLE + BROTHERS	

Word list (column):

A, ABOUT, ABOVE, ALL, ALSO, AM, AN, AND, ANY, ARRANGED, AS, AUTHORITY, BACK, BE, BEEN, BEFORE, BEING, BELIEF, BESIDE, BLACK, BLACKSMITH, BORE, BOTH, BROAD, BROTHERS, BY, CALLED, CAME, CHAPTER, CHARACTER, CHILDISH, CHRISTIAN, CONCLUSION, COULD, COUNTRY, CURLY, DARK, DAYS, DERIVED, DOWN, DREW, EACH, EARLY, EITHER, ENTERTAINED, EXCEEDINGLY, EXISTENCE, EXPLICIT, FAMILY, FANCIES, FATHER, FIRST, FIVE, FOOT, FOR, FRECKLED, FROM, GARGERY, GAVE, GEORGIANA, GET, GIVE, GRAVE, HAD, HAIR, HALF, HANDS, HAVE, HE, HIS, I, IDEA, IDENTITY, IMPRESSION, IN, INDEBTED, INFANT, INSCRIPTION, JOE, LETTERS

LIKE, LIKENESS, LITTLE, LIVING, LONG, LONGER, LOZENGES, MAKE, MAN, MARRIED, MARSH, ME, MEMORY, MILES, MINE, MORE, MOST, MOTHER, MRS, MY, MYSELF, NAME, NAMES, NEAT, NEVER, NOTHING, ODD, OF, ON, OR, OURS, OUT, PHILIP, PHOTOGRAPHS, PIP, PIRRIP, REGARDING, RELIGIOUSLY, RIVER, ROW, SACRED, SAW, SEA, SEEMS, SHAPE, SICKLY, SISTER, SO, SQUARE, STATE, STONE, STOUT, STRUGGLE, TAKEN, THAN, THAT, THE, THEIR, THEM, THEY, THINGS, THIS, TO, TOMBSTONE, TONGUE, TROUSERS-POCKETS, TRYING, TURN, TWENTY, UNIVERSAL, UNREASONABLY, UP, VIVID, WAS, WERE, WHAT, WHICH, WHO, WIFE, WITH, WITHIN, WOUND

Labels in (c): ADJ., ADV., CON., DET., NUM., PREP., PRON., PUNC., V.

(a) word frequency
(b) sentiment
(c) grammar structure

Barnbrook
www.barnbrook.net

Jonathan Barnbrook
b1966/UK

This design for *Page 1* is a mathematical, unemotional analysis of an emotive, creative text. It shows word frequency, cheekily analyses Dickens' grammar structure and uses a logical system to investigate sentiment – to alert the reader to how they are being emotionally manipulated as they read the text.

Emigre Priori Serif Regular
Emigre Priori Serif Regular Italic
Emigre Priori Sans Regular
Barnbrook, 2003

Cartlidge Levene

Col 1	Col 2	Col 3	Col 4	Col 5	Col 6	Col 7
My	Chapter	I			Pirrip	
my	father's	family			Philip	
my	name	christian			Pip	and
both	name	infant			Pip	or
nothing	tongue	longer			Pip	than
I	names	more	being		Pirrip	So
myself	father's	explicit	could		Joe	and
I	name	family	make		Gargery	as
my	authority	Mrs.	came		Georgiana	As
his	tombstone	long	be			or
my	sister	first	called			and
who	blacksmith	odd	give			and
I	father	square	married			and
my	mother	stout	saw			and
my	likeness	dark	saw			and
any	days	curly	were	of		and
either	days	black	regarding	to		and
them	photographs	childish	were	on		as
their	fancies	freckled	were	of		and
my	tombstones	sickly	like	of		and
what	shape	five	were	of		
they	letters	little	derived	of		
their	father's	stone	gave	for		
my	idea	long	was	before		
me	man	neat	drew	of		
that	hair	sacred	was	from		
he	character	five	were	of		
I	turn	little	arranged	on		
that	inscription	early	were	with		
my	Wife	universal	gave	From		
each	Above	twenty	trying	of		
which	conclusion	first	get	of		
their	mother	vivid	am	To		
mine	lozenges	broad	indebted	about		
who	foot		entertained	in		
that	half		had	beside		
I	row		been	to		
I	grave		born	of		
that	memory		had	of		
they	brothers		taken	up		
all	living		was	to		
their	struggle		wound	in		
their	belief		seems	for		
their	backs		have	on		
them	hands			with		
this	trousers-pockets			in		
Ours	state			out		
My	existence			in		
most	marsh			of		
me	country			down		
	river			by		
	river			within		
	miles			of		
	sea	the		of		
	impression	the		of		
	identity	the		of		
	things	the		to		
	1	The		to		
		the				
		the				
		the				
		the	never			an
		the	never			a
		the	unreasonably			a
		the	Also			a
		the	exceedingly			a
		the	religiously			a
		the	never			a
						a

Our *Page 1* deconstructs the text into its grammatical components and arranges it by word type as a series of lists. We found ten different classifications of words on the first page of *Great Expectations* as follows:

- proper noun
- nouns
- pronouns
- adjectives
- verbs
- adverbs
- prepositions
- conjunctions
- definite articles
- indefinite articles

Our chosen font was Helvetica Neue 55 in 7pt, set solid. Once we had classified and listed all the words, we found that we had exposed their different functions, from the expressiveness of adverbs and adjectives, to the binding functionality of conjunctions and pronouns, which act as a glue to hold the story together. We found the lists became poetic abstractions of the story, and despite their total deconstruction, still contained some remnants of the original narrative.

As infants, our brains are programmed to pick out patterns, structure and rules in the language we are exposed to. We pick up the complex grammatical rules of language in our early years. They then drift into the background as we become proficient talkers, readers and writers, allowing us to see through the complexities of grammar and sentence structure to the story itself.

Helvetica Neue 55 Roman
Linotype,
originally Haas Type Foundry
Max Miedinger, 1957
commissioned by Eduard Hoffmann
7pt set solid

Dechant Grafische Arbeiten

a

aaaaa aaaaa aaaaa aaaaa aaaa Aaaaa aaaaa aaaaa aaaaa aaaa
aaaaaa Aaa Aaaaa aaaaa aaaaa aaaaa aaaaa aaaaa aaaaa aaaa
aaaa bbbbb bbbbb bbbbb bbbbb C Ccccc ccccc ccccc ccccc
ccccc ddddd

   ddddd ddddd ddddd ddddd ddddd ddddd ddddd eeeee
eeeee eeeee eeeee eeeee eeeee eeeee eeeee eeeee eeeee
eeeee eeeee eeeee eeeee eeeee eeeee eeeee eeeee eeeee
eeeee eeee fffff fffff fffff fffff fffff fffff fff ggggg Gggggg
Ggggg ggggg ggggg hhhhh hhhhh hhhh hhhhh hhhhh
hhhhh hhhhh hhhhh hhhhh hhhhh hhhhh hhhhh hhhhh
hhhhh Iiiii iiiii iii iii Iiiii iiiii Iiiii iiii iii iii Iiiii iiiii iiiii Iii
Iiiii iiiii iiiii iiiii iiiii J kkkkk kkkkk llll llll llll llll llll llll llll
lllllll Mmmmm mmmmm mmmmmm Mmmm mmmmm
mmmmm mmmmm mmmm Mmmmm nnnnn nnnnn
nnnnn nnnnn nnnnn nnnnn nnnnn nnnnn nnnnn nnnnn
ooooo ooooo ooooo ooooo ooooo ooooo ooooo ooooo ooooo
oooo oooo Ooooo ooooooo p Pp Ppp Pp Pp Pp Ppppp pppp q
rrrrr rrrrr rrrrr rrrrr rrrrr rrrrr rrrrr rrrrr rrrrr rrrrr rrrrr rrrrr
sssss sssss sssss sssss sssss ssss sssss ssss ttttt tttt tttt ttttt
tttt tttt Ttttt tttt tttt ttt Ttttt tttt tttt tttt tttt tttt tttt tttt
ttttt ttttt uuuuu
Wwwww wwww wwwww xxx yyyyy yyyyy yyyyy yyyyy yyyyy
yyyyy yyyy z 11 '" () „„„ „„„ „„„ „„„ „„„ "" „– –

()

a a a a a a a about Above all Also am an and and and and and and and and and and and any arranged as As as authority backs be been before being belief beside black blacksmith born both broad

brothers by called called came Chapter character childish christian conclusion could country curly dark days days de- rived down drew each early either entertained exceedingly existence explicit family family fancies father father's father's father's first first five five foot for for freckled from From Gar- gery gave gave Georgiana get give grave had had hair half hands have he his I I I I I I I idea identity impression in in in in indebted infant inscription Joe letters like likeness little little living long long longer lozenges *make man married marsh me me* memory miles mine more most mother mother Mrs My my my my my my my my my my My myself name name name names neat never never never nothing odd of of of of of of of of of of of of of on on on or or Ours out Philip photographs Pip Pip Pip Pirrip Pirrip regarding religiously river river row sacred saw saw sea seems shape sickly sister So square state stone stout struggle taken than that that that that the the the The the the the the the the the the the the the their their their their their their their them them they they things this to To to to to to tombstone tombstones tongue trousers-pockets trying turn twenty

universal unreasonably up vivid was was was were were were were were what which who who Wife with with within wound 11 "" ,,,,,,,,,,,,,,,,,,,,,,,,,, ... – – –

–

Dechant Grafische Arbeiten
www.dechant.at

Susanne Dechant
b1962/Austria

As a designer of text 'landscapes', one works on the surface. Linguistic units are deconstructed, split up, divided and arranged in a comprehensible order, by which the reader's solitary path is made more secure: the purpose of this 'communication design' is to support understanding of the content, and (hopefully) even improve this understanding.

But how do we designers really deal with this process? What are the elements that make the arrangement, the guidance and the deconstruction possible? What makes the reception so smooth that the reader (thankfully) ceases to be aware of it?

To get this process on track, I had to create distance between the text and my understanding of it: I cut up, tore and uprooted it. In almost scientific steps, I sought to reach a categorical overview of the text while retaining parameters of layout and page size.

The result of the first stage is shown
on page 127. The impression is still of
a page capable of being read, even if the
linguistic logic is now broken up. Despite
this deconstruction, the content is still
decipherable because of the sentiment
engendered by the repetitive density of
certain concepts. The next progressive
steps, shown on page 126, initially split the
'molecular' words into 'atomic' letters. Now
all sense of meaning is lost, the narrative
text has given way to the rigid logic of a list.
Only the frequency of the letters offers
clues as to the language used.

But even this view seems too much of
a surface treatment. Photoshop has made
it possible to reveal the true structure of
each letter and divide it into the yes/no
of black-filled or blank pixels. Split into these
polarities, this last ordering process presents
the text at the highest possible contrast:
a blocky rectangle as the last remnant
of the message, 20% of the page covered –
80% the in-between, nothing.

Franklin-Antiqua BQ
Regular and Italic
Berthold
Günter Gerhard Lange, 1976
8.5/11pt

Morag Myerscough

chapter	both	mrs	me	neat
one	names	joe	me	row
one	nothing	gargery	an	beside
my	longer	who	odd	grave
my	or	who	idea	sacred
my	or	married	that	memory
my	more	blacksmith	that	brothers
my	explicit	never	that	mine
my	than	never	that	up
my	pip	never	he	trying
my	pip	saw	was	get
my	pip	saw	was	living
my	so	father	was	exceedingly
my	i	mother	a	early
father's	i	mother	a	universal
father's	i	any	a	struggle
father's	i	likeness	a	am
family	i	either	a	indebted
family	i	them	a	belief
name	called	them	a	religiously
name	called	for	square	entertained
name	myself	for	stout	had
being	came	their	dark	had
pirrip	to	their	man	all
pirrip	to	their	with	been
and	to	their	with	born
and	to	their	curly	backs
and	to	their	black	hands
and	to	days	hair	trousers
and	be	days	character	pockets
and	give	were	turn	taken
and	as	were	inscription	out
and	as	were	also	this
and	as	were	georgiana	state
and	on	were	wife	existence
christian	on	long	above	ours
philip	on	long	drew	marsh
infant	the	before	childish	country
tongue	the	photographs	conclusion	down
could	the	first	freckled	by
make	the	first	sickly	river
of	the	fancies	five	river
of	the	regarding	five	within
of	the	what	little	wound
of	the	they	little	twenty
of	the	they	stone	miles
of	the	like	lozenges	sea
of	the	unreasonably	each	most
of	the	derived	about	vivid
of	the	from	foot	broad
of	the	from	half	impression
of	authority	tombstones	which	identity
of	his	shape	arranged	things
of	tombstone	letters	in	seems
of	sister	gave	in	have
		gave	in	
			in	

Morag Myerscough
b1963/UK
www.supergrouplondon.co.uk
www.studiomyerscough.com

I wanted to conduct an experiment to see
how the reader/listener would understand
the text if the words were arranged in
columns, in which multiple words were
grouped together and where all punctuation
was removed. The words are listed in
the order that they appear, with multiples
shown under the word's first appearance.
There are 278 words in this piece of text
and 166 are unique. The font used is
Typewriter Condensed.

Then I read the original and my version out
loud. The former obviously flows as intended,
while in comparison my staccato version
encourages the reader to experiment with
emphasis, allowing different interpretations
of the piece.

Typewriter Condensed
Volker Busse, 2007
7/8pt

Pip.
   I give
Pirrip as
my
father's
family

from their
tombstone
s. The
shape of
the letters
on my

Chapter 1

My father's family name being Pirrip, and my Christian name Philip, my infant tongue could make of both nothing longer or more explicit than Pip. So, I called myself Pip, and came to be called Pip.

I give Pirrip as my father's family name, on the authority of his tombstone and my sister – Mrs. Joe Gargery, who married the blacksmith. As I never saw my father or my mother, and never saw any likeness of either of them (for their days were long before the days of photographs), my first fancies regarding what they were like, were unreasonably derived from their tombstones. The shape of the letters on my father's, gave me an odd idea that he was a square, stout, dark man, with curly black hair. From the character and turn of the inscription, *"Also Georgiana Wife of the Above,"* I drew a childish conclusion that my mother was freckled and sickly. To five little stone lozenges, each about a foot and a half long, which were arranged in a neat row beside their grave, and were sacred to the memory of five little brothers of mine – who gave up trying to get a living, exceedingly early in that universal struggle – I am indebted for a belief I religiously entertained that they had all been born on their backs with their hands in their trousers-pockets, and had never taken them out in this state of existence.

Ours was the marsh country, down by the river, within, as the river wound, twenty miles of the sea. My first most vivid and broad impression of the identity of things, seems to

abc—xyz
www.abc-xyz.co.uk

Julian Morey
b1966/UK

If Charles Dickens had been alive today
he would have no doubt written about all
the ills of our modern society; the bankers,
the B-list celebrities and the hoodies.
He would have no doubt published
his narratives through the latest forms
of communication; the Internet, the
smartphone and the eReader. The story
remains the same, however the medium
is now forever changing.

Helvetica Neue 65 Medium
Linotype,
originally Haas Type Foundry
Max Miedinger, 1957
commissioned by Eduard Hoffmann
size variable

Neil Donnelly

My father's family name being Pirrip

AND MY CHRISTIAN NAME PHILIP

MY infant tongue could make of both names nothing longer or more explicit than Pip.

So, I called myself Pip, and came to be called Pip.

I give Pirrip as my father's family name, on the authority of his tombstone and my sister – Mrs. Joe Gargery, who married the blacksmith. As I never saw my father or my mother, and never saw any likeness of either of them (for their days were long before the days of photographs), my first fancies regarding what they were like, were unreasonably derived from their tombstones. The shape of the letters on my father's, gave me an odd idea that he was a square, stout, dark man, with curly black hair. From the character and turn of the inscription, "*Also Georgiana Wife of the Above,*" I drew a childish conclusion that my mother was freckled and sickly. To five little stone lozenges, each about a foot and a half long, which were arranged in a neat row beside their grave, and were sacred to the memory of five little brothers of mine – who gave up trying to get a living, exceedingly early in that universal struggle – I am indebted for a belief I religiously entertained that they had all been born on their backs with their hands in their trousers-pockets, and had never taken them out in this state of existence.

Ours

Was the marsh country, down by the river, within, as the river wound, twenty miles of the sea. My first most vivid and broad impression of the identity of things, seems to me to have

Neil Donnelly
b 1977/USA
www.neildonnelly.net

This cheap edition of my books is dedicated
to the English people, in whose approval,
if the books be true in spirit, they will live,
and out of whose memory, if they be false,
they will very soon die.

Charles Dickens
in a discarded dedication to an
inexpensive serial edition of his works
published in 1846

The Life of Charles Dickens: 1812–1842
John Forster

Tempo Heavy Condensed
Linotype
Robert Hunter Middleton, 1931

Univers 75 Black
Linotype,
originally Deberny & Peignot
Adrian Frutiger, 1957

Neue Helvetica 65 Medium
Neue Helvetica 93 Black Extended
Linotype,
originally Haas Type Foundry
Max Miedinger, 1957
commissioned by Eduard Hoffmann

ITC Franklin Gothic Demi
International Typeface Corporation
Morris Fuller Benton for
American Type Founders, 1904
Victor Caruso, 1980

Body text
Imperial
Roman and Italic
Bitstream
Ed Shaar (Intertype), 1957
7.25/8pt

Experimental Jetset

My father's family name being _____ ,
and my christian name _____ ,
my infant tongue could make of both names
nothing longer or more explicit than _____ .

So, I called myself _____ ,
and came to be called _____ .

I give _____
as my father's family name, on the
authority of his tombstone and my sister _____ ,
who married _____ .

As I never saw my father or my mother, and
never saw any likeness of either of them (for
their days were long before the days of
photographs), my first fancies regarding what
they were like, were unreasonably derived
from their tombstones.
The shape of the letters on my father's, gave
me an odd idea that he was a _____ ,
_____ ,
_____ man
with _____ hair.

From the character and turn of the inscription, "_____
_____ ",
I drew a childish conclusion
that my mother was _____ and
_____ .

To _____
little stone lozenges, each about _____ ft. long,
which were arranged in a neat row beside their
grave, and were sacred to the memory of _____
little brothers of mine – who gave up trying to
get a living, exceedingly early in that universal
struggle – I am indebted for a belief I religiously
entertained that they had all been born on their
backs with their hands in their
trousers-pockets, and had never taken them
out in this state of existence.

Ours was the marsh country, down by the river,
within, as the river wound _____ miles
of the sea.
My first most vivid and broad impression of the
identity of things, seems to me to have

Experimental Jetset
www.experimentaljetset.nl

Erwin Brinkers
b1973/The Netherlands

Danny van den Dungen
b1971/The Netherlands

Marieke Stolk
b1967/The Netherlands

What particularly struck us about the first few paragraphs of *Great Expectations* was the idea of young Pip trying to gather an image of his deceased father, mother and five siblings, based on the inscriptions and shapes of the letterforms on their gravestones. In a way, Pip is attempting to fill in the blanks of his orphaned life.

To emphasise the tragic quality of this attempt, we decided to use this idea of filling in blanks (or filling out blanks), and we tried to do this by turning our design for *Page 1* into a form, not unlike a 'boilerplate' legal document.

We appreciate that this may seem a sarcastic or even cynical gesture, but our intention is the complete opposite. Our typographic exercise does not suggest that every piece of literature can be turned into a bureaucratic form, but instead we want to suggest that every bureaucratic form has a narrative dimension, as well as a tragic potential.

▬▬▬▬▬▬▬▬▬▬▬▬▬▬

The dimensions of the page, the choice
of typeface (and type size) follow quite
naturally from the concept. Obviously, this
typographic experiment should be seen
for what it is: a mere exercise. In no way are
we proposing that our interpretation is
the ideal way to typeset the whole of this
particular novel. But within the context of this
brief, we felt it would be interesting to opt
for a more subjective interpretation of the
text – one might argue that there is no such
thing as an 'objective' interpretation anyway.

▬▬▬▬▬▬▬▬▬▬▬▬▬▬

Helvetica Neue 55 Roman
Helvetica Neue 75 Bold
Linotype,
originally Haas Type Foundry
Max Miedinger, 1957
commissioned by Eduard Hoffmann
7.5/8.5pt

Oded Ezer

English   Korean   Hebrew

Chapter 1

Family name was Firif and my first name - Philip. Childish tongue, trying to merge these two names, not smart enough to design a better phrase than "Pip". I called myself Pip, and thanks to the fertile imagination were all behind me.

I never saw my parents, nor his portraits, because those days have not had a form of photography. First I thought childish about my parents, who lacked any basis in reality, was born in my mind under the influence of tombstones on the graves. Monument to my father made me, for some reason, the assumption that surprising, the man was a large man, whose body is solid and curly hair. Address "as well as Georgiana", which was engraved on the monument to my mother, she pushed me childish conclusion that my mother was a sickly, yellow-faced and freckled. Five tiny tombstones in memory of my little brothers, who stood in line with the tombstones of my parents, gave me the Sabra, the brothers were born in supine position, and Cscfot hands in his pockets trousers, of which no longer took us all the days of their short lives on earth.

My native district, he was inclined swamps, lay on the shores of the river, to twenty miles from the sea. First defined the concept of the world around me, was born in

✓

New! Click the words above to view alternate translations. Dismiss

Oded Ezer
b1972/Israel
www.odedezer.com

In its Wikipedia entry, Google Translate is described as 'a free statistical machine translation service provided by Google Inc. to translate a section of text, document or webpage, into another language'.

During the last century, Charles Dickens' *Great Expectations* was translated from English to Hebrew, my mother tongue, in a number of editions. I selected a 1955 translation (by K Katsenelson) and using Google Translate converted it back into its 'original' English. The result is not only aesthetically and typographically poor, it is also totally incorrect, turning the classic text into an unreadable, clumsy one.

In undertaking this, I hope to question the relationships between major international languages (such as English) and 'provincial' ones (such as Hebrew); between aesthetics of printed matter and aesthetics of the screen; between 'good' and 'bad' typography; between 'originality' and 'imitation' – and between man and machine.

Ed Harrison

```
<head>
   <meta http-equiv="Content-Type"
    content="application/xhtml+xml; charset=utf-8"/>
   <title>Great Expectations</title>
   <link rel="stylesheet" href="css/main.css" />
</head>

<h1>Chapter I</h1>

<p>My father's family name being Pirrip, and my
christian name Philip, my infant tongue could make
of both names nothing longer or more explicit than
Pip. So, I called myself Pip, and came to be called
Pip.</p>
<p>I give Pirrip as my father's family name, on the
authority of his tombstone and my sister — Mrs. Joe
Gargery, who married the blacksmith. As I never saw
my father or my mother, and never saw any likeness
of either of them (for their days were long before
the days of photographs), my first fancies regarding
what they were like, were unreasonably derived from
their tombstones. The shape of the letters on my
father's, gave me an odd idea that he was a square,
stout, dark man, with curly black hair. From the
character and turn of the inscription, "Also
Georgiana Wife of the Above," I drew a childish
conclusion that my mother was freckled and sickly.
To five little stone lozenges, each about a foot
and a half long, which were arranged in a neat row
beside their grave, and were sacred to the
memory of five little brothers of mine — who gave up
trying to get a living, exceedingly early in that
universal struggle — I am indebted for a belief I
religiously entertained that they had all been born
on their backs with their hands in their trousers-
pockets, and had never taken them out in this
state of existence.</p>
<p>Ours was the marsh country, down by the river,
within, as the river wound, twenty miles of the
sea. My first most vivid and broad impression of the
identity of things, seems to me to have been gained
```

Ed Harrison
b1989/UK
www.edharrisondesign.com

BA Graphic Design student
University of Brighton
UK

I laid out my design for *Page 1* in the same coding language used to create digital eBooks. I chose to use Courier because it's the default typeface used in XML and HTML coding programs.

My intention was to reveal a 'behind the scenes' view of an eBook while displaying it in a way that mimicked the layout of a traditional printed page.

Dickens' stories retain their popularity and will remain with us, no matter what format the books take.

Courier Regular
Monotype
Howard Kettler, 1955
8/11pt

Jo Hawkes

CHAPTER I

MY FATHER'S FAMILY NAME BEING PIRRIP, AND MY CHRISTIAN NAME PHILIP, MY INFANT TONGUE COULD MAKE OF BOTH NAMES NOTHING LONGER OR MORE EXPLICIT THAN PIP. SO, I CALLED MYSELF PIP, AND CAME TO BE CALLED PIP.

I GIVE PIRRIP AS MY FATHER'S FAMILY NAME, ON THE AUTHORITY OF HIS TOMBSTONE AND MY SISTER – MRS. JOE GARGERY, WHO MARRIED THE BLACKSMITH. AS I NEVER SAW MY FATHER OR MY MOTHER, AND NEVER SAW ANY LIKENESS OF EITHER OF THEM (FOR THEIR DAYS WERE LONG BEFORE THE DAYS OF PHOTOGRAPHS), MY FIRST FANCIES REGARDING WHAT THEY WERE LIKE, WERE UNREASONABLY DERIVED FROM THEIR TOMBSTONES. THE SHAPE OF THE LETTERS ON MY FATHER'S, GAVE ME AN ODD IDEA THAT HE WAS A SQUARE, STOUT, DARK MAN, WITH CURLY BLACK HAIR. FROM THE CHARACTER AND TURN OF THE INSCRIPTION, "ALSO GEORGIANA WIFE OF THE ABOVE," I DREW A CHILDISH CONCLUSION THAT MY MOTHER WAS FRECKLED AND SICKLY. TO FIVE LITTLE STONE LOZENGES, EACH ABOUT A FOOT AND A HALF LONG, WHICH WERE ARRANGED IN A NEAT ROW BESIDE THEIR GRAVE, AND WERE SACRED TO THE MEMORY OF FIVE LITTLE BROTHERS OF MINE – WHO GAVE UP TRYING TO GET A LIVING, EXCEEDINGLY EARLY IN THAT UNIVERSAL STRUGGLE – I AM INDEBTED FOR A BELIEF I RELIGIOUSLY ENTERTAINED THAT THEY HAD ALL BEEN BORN ON THEIR BACKS WITH THEIR HANDS IN THEIR TROUSERS-POCKETS, AND HAD NEVER TAKEN THEM OUT IN THIS STATE OF EXISTENCE.

OURS WAS THE MARSH COUNTRY, DOWN BY THE RIVER, WITHIN, AS THE RIVER WOUND, TWENTY MILES OF THE SEA. MY FIRST MOST VIVID AND BROAD IMPRESSION OF THE IDENTITY OF THINGS, SEEMS TO ME TO HAVE

Jo Hawkes
b1989/UK
www.johawkes.com
www.johawkesdesign.blogspot.com

BA Graphic Design student
Kingston University, London
UK

Modern life is often rushed and hectic.
Even when reading novels for pleasure,
we can feel pressured to get to the end
as quickly as possible due to other daily
commitments. Traditionally, novels are left
aligned, in upper and lowercase serif fonts
for optimum ease of reading. I wanted to
lay out the text in a way that would slow our
reading down, so that we are forced to fully
absorb every word of this celebrated novel.

It is generally recognised that eye tracking
is affected by page layout and by the fonts
used. So, I researched how to slow and
inhibit reading. By increasing the leading
and using large paragraph spaces, the reader
is forced to move gradually down the page,
while the right alignment makes 'speed
reading' almost impossible and slows the
pace even more. I set the text in all caps,
destroying the word shapes, making word
recognition slower and therefore making
rereading more frequent.

I used the font Monotype Grotesque as it is
an older sans serif but is contemporary in
feel. Like *Great Expectations*, it is timeless.
Serif fonts are also considered easier on
the eye for continuous text and so this font
impedes the reader further. The body text
is set in 6pt Light, also used to discourage
speed reading.

Glossary
sans serif
serif

Monotype Grotesque Light
Frank Pierpont, 1926
6/10pt

Yu Jin Kang

Yu Jin Kang
b1987/South Korea/UK
www.gobbiekoko.blogspot.com/

BA Graphic Design student
Kingston University, London
UK

Unlike many contemporary novels,
Great Expectations was first published in
serial form, from December 1860 to August
1861. Moreover, even up to the present
day, the book has never been out of print.
In my opinion, this longevity seems somehow
at odds with the immediacy of today's
digital age.

Taking inspiration from the terms 'serial'
and 'analogue' I have chosen to create
a QR code for *Page 1*. When this is scanned
using a mobile phone QR reader, the viewer
is taken to the Notes page on their phone,
where they will find the text from the first
page of the novel transcribed in the default
font and style of the notes app. By translating
the original book into digital form in this
way, I wish to highlight how the details and
beauty of a book are lost via the immediacy
of some modern technology.

QR codes are popular due to their large
storage capacity and the speed at which they
can be read. I found that I needed to design
more than one QR code to contain all the
text and that the complexity of the design
made it slower for the scanner to read. This
also produced some unexpected results –
sometimes the QR reading of my designs
took me to a completely different product,
underlining the lack of permanency that
this digital format provides.

Marcus Leis Allion

CHAPTER ONE

My father's family name being *Pirrip*, and my Christian name *Philip*, my infant tongue could make of both names nothing longer or more explicit than *Pip*. So, I called myself *Pip*, and came to be called *Pip*.

I give *Pirrip* as my father's family name, on the authority of his tombstone and my sister,—Mrs. Joe Gargery, who married the blacksmith. As I never saw my father or my mother, and never saw any likeness of either of them (for their days were long before the days of photographs), my first fancies regarding what they were like, were unreasonably derived from their tombstones. The shape of the letters on my father's, gave me an odd idea that he was a square, stout, dark man, with curly black hair. From the character and turn of the inscription, "Also Georgiana *Wife of the Above*," I drew a childish conclusion that my mother was freckled and sickly. To five little stone lozenges, each about a foot and a half long, which were arranged in a neat row beside their grave, and were sacred to the memory of five little brothers of mine,—who gave up trying to get a living, exceedingly early in that universal struggle,—I am indebted for a belief I religiously entertained that they had all been born on their backs with their hands in their trousers-pockets, and had never taken them out in this state of existence.

Ours was the marsh country, down by the river, within, as the river wound, twenty miles of the sea. My first impression of the identity of things seems to me to have

Marcus Leis Allion
b1973/UK
WWW.u-n-d-t.COM

My *Page 1* design corresponds to
the structure of Dickens' manuscript but
replaces the handwritten forms with a
number of different typefaces. The all caps,
fixed-width typeface is a reference to
the early developments of the typewriter,
a technology that was on the cusp
of transforming the process of writing
by the 1860s. The scrawled out parts
of the manuscript are represented through
the use of typographic ornament, as
detailed opposite.

I was interested in foregrounding the impact
that different technologies and materials
have, not only on how we interpret a text,
but also on their capacity to inform its
construction. For example, if one is using
pen and ink it is much easier to cross out
a mistake than to try and delete it. Our
writing tools then are not simply instruments
directed by an author, but are active agents
in the work, enabling certain actions while
limiting others.

Three figures who have greatly informed
my own practice, and this design in
particular, sadly passed away in 2011:
the artist Richard Hamilton, Steve Jobs
of Apple and the media theorist Friedrich
Kittler. This design is dedicated to them
and their work. I would also like to thank
David Wright, Curator of the Wisbech and
Fenland Museum, for supplying me with
an image of Dickens' original manuscript.

**What remains of people is what media
can store and communicate.**

Friedrich Kittler
Gramophone, Film, Typewriter
Stanford University Press, 1999

Bickham Script Pro
Adobe
Richard Lipton, 1997

Bodoni Ornaments
Linotype
Sumner Stone, 1994
after Giambattista Bodoni c1798

Britannic Bold
URW++
URW Design Studio, 1985
original by Stephenson Blake, 1901

Comb Pro Thin
OurType
Frederik Berlaen, 2010

Engravers MT
Monotype
after Robert Wiebking, 1899

Fakt Medium
OurType
Thomas Thiemich, 2010

Wilhelm Klingspor Gotisch
Linotype
after Rudolf Koch, 1925

Paul Luna

"THE STORY OF OUR LIVES FROM YEAR TO YEAR."—Shak

ALL THE YEAR ROU

A WEEKLY JOURNAL.

CONDUCTED BY CHARLES DICKENS

WITH WHICH IS INCORPORATED HOUSEHOLD

Nᵒ. 84.]   SATURDAY, DECEMBER 1, 1860.

GREAT EXPECTATIONS.

BY CHARLES DICKENS.

CHAPTER I.

My father's family name being Pirrip, and my christian name Philip, my infant tongue could make of both names nothing longer or more explicit than Pip. So, I called myself Pip, and came to be called Pip.

I give Pirrip as my father's family name, on the authority of his tombstone and my sister—Mrs. Joe Gargery, who married the blacksmith. As I never saw my father or my mother, and never saw any likeness of either of them (for their days were long before the days of photographs), my first fancies regarding what they were like, were unreasonably derived from their tombstones. The shape of the letters on my father's, gave me an odd idea that he was a square, stout, dark man, with curly black hair. From the character and turn of the inscription, " *Also Georgiana Wife of the Above*," I drew a childish conclusion that my mother was freckled and sickly. To five little stone lozenges, each about a foot and a half long, which were arranged in a neat row beside their grave, and were sacred to the memory of five little brothers of mine—who gave up trying to get a living, exceedingly early in that universal struggle—I am indebted for a belief I religiously entertained that they had all been born on their backs with their hands in their trousers-pockets, and had never taken them out in this state of existence.

Ours was the marsh country, down by the river, within, as the river wound, twenty miles of the sea. My first most vivid and broad im-

and that the distant savage l
wind was rushing, was the
small bundle of shivers grow
and beginning to cry, was P
"Hold your noise!" cried
a man started up from amon
side of the church porch.
little devil, or I'll cut your t
A fearful man, all in coarse
iron on his leg. A man wit
broken shoes, and with an o
his head. A man who had be
and smothered in mud, and la
cut by flints, and stung by n
briars; who limped, and sh
and growled; and whose teet
head as he seized me by the
"O! Don't cut my throat,
terror. "Pray don't do it, s
"Tell us your name!"
"Quick!"
"Pip, sir."
"Once more," said the m
"Give it mouth!"
"Pip. Pip, sir."
"Show us where you liv
"Pint out the place!"
I pointed to where our vill
in-shore among the alder-tree
mile or more from the church
The man, after looking at
turned me upside-down, and e
There was nothing in them bu
When the church came to its
sudden and strong that he ma
heels before me, and I saw th
legs—when the church came
was seated on a high tombston
he ate the bread ravenously.

Paul Luna
b1952/UK
www.lunascafe.org

If you look at the original serial publication
of Dickens' novels, you'll see something
of his world in the graphic presentation.
The stories are chopped into weekly chunks
and surrounded by advertisements for
cut-price tailors and mourning emporiums.
The reader is reminded that 'the new serial
story, *GREAT EXPECTATIONS*, by CHARLES
DICKENS, is continued from week to week
until completed in August'. Your weekly fix
is assured for nigh on nine months. You are
immersed in the story.

The first chapter of *Great Expectations* is
a *tour de force*, and must have been planned
exactly to fit the format of *All The Year Round*.
It occupies two complete pages and the
final paragraph is 'bumped' to fill the last line.

The pervading tone of the first column
is bleakness, death and misperception.
Pip doesn't know his parents, but invents
their personalities from the engraved
letterforms on their tombstones – no doubt
a square Doric for his father and a rather
weak, spotty Italic for his mother. But the plot
has to develop and Magwitch appears with
a bang at the top of the second column.
We are not even 500 words into the story,
and a violent cut-throat has appeared!
The language switches from introspection
to short, violent exchanges, and the reader
is hooked before the turn of the page.

Glossary
Doric [type]
line-break
Modern [type]

In my design for *Page 1*, I wanted to show
something of the reader's response as
the story grows to occupy their thoughts,
and the surrounding noise of the busy
magazine page fades away. I used Bitstream
De Vinne Text and modified the weight to
match the Modern of the original publication;
Monotype Victoria Titling is a close match to
the titling face used. I followed the house-
style and line-breaks of the original exactly.

Titling
Monotype Victoria Condensed Titling
Monotype Type Drawing Office

Body text
De Vinne Text
Bitstream
Gustav F Schroeder, 1890
8.4pt set solid

Ellen Lupton

charlesD Charles Dickens

a foot and a half long, which were arranged in a neat row beside their grave, and were sacred to the memory of five little brothers of mine

December 1, 1860

---

charlesD Charles Dickens

Georgiana Wife of the Above," I drew a childish conclusion that my mother was freckled and sickly. To five little stone lozenges, each about

December 1, 1860

---

charlesD Charles Dickens

gave me an odd idea that he was a square, stout, dark man, with curly black hair. From the character and turn of the inscription, "Also

December 1, 1860

---

charlesD Charles Dickens

my first fancies regarding what they were like, were unreasonably derived from their tombstones. The shape of the letters on my father's,

December 1, 1860

---

charlesD Charles Dickens

As I never saw my father or my mother, and never saw any likeness of them (for their days were long before the days of photographs),

December 1, 1860

---

charlesD Charles Dickens

I give Pirrip as my father's family name, on the authority of his tomb-stone and my sister–Mrs. Joe Gargery, who married the blacksmith.

December 1, 1860

---

charlesD Charles Dickens

my infant tongue could make of both names nothing longer or more explicit than Pip. So, I called myself Pip, and came to be called Pip.

December 1, 1860

---

charlesD Charles Dickens

My father's family name being Pirrip, and my christian name Philip,

December 1, 1860

Ellen Lupton
b1963/USA
www.elupton.com
www.thinkingwithtype.com

Charles Dickens enjoyed tremendous celebrity during his lifetime. He worked hard to build a personal relationship with his readers, sometimes devoting more time to his speaking tours than to his writing. Dickens owned the journal in which he first published *Great Expectations*, an arrangement that enriched him greatly.

As editor and publisher, he was able to nurture the work of his contemporaries and to promote favoured political causes as well as maintain a lucrative vehicle for his own literary output. Dickens would likely have enjoyed the many tools available to authors today, including the ability to disseminate a novel over time – not just in single chapters, but in 140-character increments.

**Aaron Merrigan
Fred North**

to

Ours   the   country,   by   river,   as   river ,   twenty
of   sea.   first   vivid   broad   of   identity   things,   to

they   all   born   their   with   hands   their   -pockets,   had
taken   out   this   of   .

in   universal   –   I   indebted   a   I   entertained
of   little   of   –   who   up   to   a   exceedingly
half ,   which   arranged   a   row   their ,   and   sacred   the
mother   freckled   sickly.   five   stone ,   each   a   and
of   Above,"   "Georgiana   drew   childish   that
he   a   ,   stout,   man,   curly   hair.   The   inscription,"
their   of   letters   my   ,   gave   an   idea
never   any   of   of   (for   days   long   of   the   of
),   my   fancies   were   what   were ,   were   derived
Joe   –   who ,   the   .   As   never   my   or   mother,
I   Pirrip   my   family ,   on   authority   his   sister   and

,   and   to   called   .

make   both   nothing   or   explicit   Pip. ,   I   myself
father's   name   Pirrip,   my   name   ,   my   tongue

CHAPTER 1

My   family   being   ,   and   christian   Philip,   infant
could   of   names   longer   more   than   .   So,   called
Pip,   came   be   Pip.

give   as   father's   name,   the   of   tombstone   my
–   Mrs.   Gargery,   married   blacksmith.   I   saw   father   my   ,
and   saw   likeness   either   them   (their   were   before   days
photographs),   first   regarding   they   like,   unreasonably
from   tombstones.   shape   the   on   father's,   me   odd   that
was   square,   ,   dark   ,   with   black   .   From   character   turn
the   ,   "Also   Wife   the   ,"   I   a   conclusion
my   was   and   .   To   little   lozenges,   about   foot   a
long,   were   in   neat   beside   grave,   were   to
memory   five   brothers   mine   –   gave   trying   get   living,
early   that   struggle   –   am   for   belief   religiously   that
had   been   on   backs   their   in   trousers-   ,   and
never   them   in   state   existence.

was   marsh   ,   down   the   ,   within,   the   wound,   miles
the   .   My   most   and   impression   the   of   ,   seems
me   have

Aaron Merrigan
b1989/UK
www.aaronmerrigan.co.uk

Fred North
b1990/UK
www.frednorth.co.uk

BA Graphic Design students
Kingston University, London
UK

Our *Page 1* design is a 'two-person book'.
We have assumed that to tempt people into
buying a traditional book, rather than an
eBook, we needed to incorporate a 'gimmick'.
Set in Meta Pro, this design is impossible to
read on your own, giving a new twist to the
term 'interactive'. It addresses the solitary
nature of reading a novel by introducing the
need for teamwork. Sitting opposite one
another, each person alternates reading
a word aloud, making every reading unique.

Chapter heading
FF Meta Pro Medium
FontFont
Erik Spiekermann, 1991
9.5pt

Body text
FF Meta Pro Regular
FontFont
Erik Spiekermann, 1991
6.65/9.5pt

MuirMcNeil Design Systems

ALL THE YEAR R

A WEEKLY JOURNAL.

CONDUCTED BY CHARLES DIC

WITH WHICH IS INCORPORATED HOUSE

Nº. 84.]　　　　SATURDAY, DECEMBER 1, 1860.

GREAT EXPECTATIONS.

BY CHARLES DICKENS.

CHAPTER I.

My father's family name being Pirrip, and my christian name Philip, my infant tongue could make of both names nothing longer or more explicit than Pip. So, I called myself Pip, and came to be called Pip.

I give Pirrip as my father's family name, on the authority of his tombstone and my sister—Mrs. Joe Gargery, who married the blacksmith. As I never saw my father or my mother, and never saw any likeness of either of them (for their days were long before the days of photographs), my first fancies regarding what they were like, were unreasonably derived from their tombstones. The shape of the letters on my father's, gave me an odd idea that he was a square, stout, dark man with curly black hair. From the character and turn of the inscription, "*Also Georgiana Wife of the Above,*" I drew a childish conclusion that my mother was freckled and sickly. To five little stone lozenges, each about a foot and a half long, which were arranged in a neat row beside their grave, and were sacred to the memory of five little brothers of mine—who gave up trying to get a living, exceedingly early in that universal struggle—I am indebted for a belief I religiously entertained that they had all been born on their backs with their hands in their trousers-pockets, and had never taken them out in this state of existence.

Ours was the marsh country, down by the river, within, as the river wound, twenty miles of the sea. My first most vivid and broad impression of the identity of things, seems to me to have

and that the dista
wind was rushing
small bundle of sh
and beginning to

"Hold your noi
a man started up
side of the chur
little devil, or I'll

A fearful man, a
iron on his leg.
broken shoes, and
his head. A man
and smothered in
cut by flints, and
briars; who limpe
and growled; and
head as he seized n

"O! Don't cut
terror. "Pray do
"Tell us you
"Quick!"

"Pip, sir."

"Once more,"
"Give it mouth!"

"Pip. Pip, sir

"Show us whe
"Pint out the pla

I pointed to wh
in-shore among th
mile or more from

The man, after
turned me upside-d
There was nothing
When the church
sudden and strong
heels before me, a
legs—when the c
was seated on a hig
he ate the bread r

"You young de

MuirMcNeil Design Systems
www.muirmcneil.com

Paul McNeil
b1955/UK

The brief for the *Page 1* project asks
contributors to provide a rationale for their
design, indicating their choice of typefaces
used. This seems to suggest that such
decisions are among the most significant
ones in the design of printed pages for
narrative fiction. These days, I'm not so sure.

Beatrice Warde's well-worn metaphor
for book typography as a 'crystal goblet'
designed to 'reveal rather than to conceal'
is perhaps less direct and more easily
misunderstood as modernist elitism than her
later propositions comparing the effective
layout of the book page to the construction
of a window frame. This brings ideas about
design as performance and representation
into sharp perspective, reflecting, as it does,
on the subtle interconnectedness of the
view, the frame and the viewer. Language,
as Mel Bochner said, is not transparent.

For the *Page 1* project, I've been more
interested in working with these ideas than
with my personal preferences in the choice
of nuts and bolts.

Initially, I took the opportunity to research
a number of first pages from several
early editions of *Great Expectations* and
I experimented with a series of alternative
designs that overlaid the various type
areas and formats proportionately on the
page. However, I soon realised that this
approach emphasised the material qualities
of the frame over the view it provided.

When I discovered the first edition of the novel in its original serialised form, this immediately struck me as sufficient for the project brief and for what I wanted to do: to make a statement about the purpose of typography as the *performance* of a text in both the theatrical and functional senses of that word. The final page design presented here is a carefully positioned facsimile of the original 1860 edition, with a few subtle modifications. Its (apparently) authentic Dickensian content and context demonstrate an attempt to respond to the *Page 1* brief faithfully – although I am still a little unsure of the typefaces used!

Moa Pårup

CHAPTER I

My father's family name being Pirrip, and my christian name Philip, my infant tongue could make of both names nothing longer or more explicit than Pip. So, I called myself Pip, and came to be called Pip.

I give Pirrip as my father's family name, on the authority of his tombstone and my sister — Mrs. Joe Gargery, who married the blacksmith. As I never saw my father or my mother, and never saw any likeness of either of them (for their days were long before the days of photographs), my first fancies regarding what they were like, were unreasonably derived from their tombstones. The shape of the letters on my father's, gave me an odd idea that he was a square, stout, dark man, with curly black hair. From the character and turn of the inscription, *"Also Georgiana Wife of the Above,"* I drew a childish conclusion that my mother was freckled and sickly. To five little stone lozenges, each about a foot and a half long, which were arranged in a neat row beside their grave, and were sacred to the memory of five little brothers of mine — who gave up trying to get a living, exceedingly early in that universal struggle — I am indebted for a belief I religiously entertained that they had all been born on their backs with their hands in their trousers-pockets, and had never taken them out in this state of existence.

Ours was the marsh country, down by the river, within, as the river wound, twenty miles of the sea. My first most vivid and broad impression of the identity of things, seems to me to have

Moa Pårup
b1982/Sweden
www.moaparup.com

MA Visual Communication student
Royal College of Art, London
UK

Great Expectations, along with many of Charles Dickens' other novels, was not originally published as such. Instead, his stories were published as serials, with readers receiving a new episode every week or month. By using this format they became affordable and accessible to a wider audience. This non-elitist means of publishing seems to be in keeping with Dickens' engagement with social issues. Choosing an episodical form of writing also allowed him to alter the story in response to audience reaction, and he often redrafted texts as they were being published.

If Charles Dickens were alive today he would probably use electronic publishing in order to reach a broad audience. Using the Internet as a forum for political and social debate would provide him with comment and reaction that would then in turn inform his writing.

Georgia
Regular and Italic
Microsoft
Matthew Carter, 1996
8/13.279pt

Research Studios

MY FATHER'S family name being Pirrip, and my christian name Philip,

my infant tongue could make of both names nothing longer or more explicit than Pip.

So, I called myself Pip,

I give Pirrip as my father's family name, on the authority of his tombstone and

and came to be called Pip.

my sister Mrs. Joe Gargery, who married the

BLACKSMITH.

As I never saw my father or my mother, and never saw any likeness of either of them (for their days were long before the days of photographs), my first fancies regarding what they were like, were unreasonably derived from their tombstones.

The shape of the letters on my father's, gave me an odd idea that he was a square, stout, dark man, with curly black hair. From the character and turn of the inscription, "Also Georgiana Wife of the Above," I drew a childish conclusion that my mother was freckled and sickly. To five little stone lozenges, each about a foot and a half long, which were arranged in a neat row beside their grave, and were sacred to the

memory of five little brothers of mine

– who gave up trying to get a living, exceedingly early in that universal struggle –

I am indebted for a belief I religiously entertained that they had all been born on their backs with their hands in their trousers-pockets, and had never taken them out in this state of existence.

Ours was the marsh country,

down by the river, within, as the river wound, twenty miles of the sea.

My first most vivid and broad impression of the identity of things, seems to me to have been

Research Studios
www.researchstudios.com

Tom Balchin
b1987/UK

I find that my train of thought can easily drift when I read. I often 'read' the words but am thinking about other things at the same time, and these breaks in concentration mean that I miss parts of the narrative. In my design for *Page 1* I wanted to provide 'thought punctuation' that lends visual rhythm to the text to help prevent this from happening.

I decided to highlight these parts of the text:

- the introduction of the protagonist
- the introduction of the setting
- the background of the protagonist
- the introduction of other primary characters

I wanted to explore whether the classical conventions of book typography are becoming less relevant, determined as they were in part by earlier typesetting methods. The increase in digital publishing could mean that more personalised reading experiences are possible, and it is this that I have experimented with in my layout of this text. Joanna is my chosen font because it works well at all scales and so is suited to my design.

Joanna Book
Monotype
Eric Gill, 1937

Spin

×

Chapter
O1

My father's family name being Pirrip, and my christian name Philip, my infant tongue could make of both names nothing longer or more explicit than Pip.

So, I called myself Pip, and came to be called Pip.

I give Pirrip as my father's name, on the authority of his…

tombstone and my sister – Mrs. Joe Gargery, who married the blacksmith.

As I never saw my father or my mother, and never saw any likeness of either of them (**for their days were long before the days of photographs**), my first fancies regarding what they were like, were unreasonably derived from their tombstones. The shape of the letters on my father's, gave me an odd idea that he was a square, stout, dark man, with curly black hair.

From the character and turn of the inscription, "Also Georgiana Wife of the Above," I drew a childish conclusion that my mother was freckled and sickly.

To five little stone lozenges, each about a foot and a half long, which were arranged in a neat row beside their grave, and were sacred to the memory of five little brothers of mine – who gave up trying to get a living, exceedingly early in that universal struggle

Spin
www.spin.co.uk

Tony Brook
b1962/UK

Claudia Klat
b1983/Switzerland

Our *Page 1* design imagines how, since *Great Expectations* was first published, the text has travelled across time and continents, through different fashions of book design and different cultural typographic stylings, all the while being read in very different contexts to the one in which it was written. Yet through all its travels, the power of the novel's story has not been lost.

Blado Italic
Monotype
Ludovico degli Arrighi, c1526

Fette Fraktur Regular
Bauer Type Foundry
Johann Christian Bauer, 1850

Times New Roman Regular
Monotype
Stanley Morison,
Victor Lardent, 1932

Albertus Roman
Monotype
Berthold Wolpe, 1938

Univers 55 Roman
Linotype,
originally Deberny & Peignot
Adrian Frutiger, 1957

ITC Elan Book
Albert Boton, 1985

OCRB Medium
Monotype
Adrian Frutiger, 1968

David Sudlow

Chapter 1

My father's family name being Pirrip,
and my christian name Philip,
my infant tongue could make of both names nothing longer
or more explicit
than Pip.
So, I called myself Pip,
and came to be called Pip.

I give Pirrip as my father's family name,
on the authority of his tombstone and my sister –
Mrs. Joe Gargery,
who married the blacksmith.
As I never saw my father or my mother,
and never saw any likeness of either of them
(for their days were long before the days of photographs),
my first fancies regarding what they were like,
were unreasonably derived from their tombstones.

The shape of the letters on my father's,
gave me an odd idea that he was a square,
stout,
dark man,
with curly black hair.
From the character and turn of the inscription,
'Also Georgiana Wife of the Above,'
I drew a childish conclusion
that my mother was freckled and sickly.

To five little stone lozenges,
each about a foot and a half long,
which were arranged in a neat row beside their grave,
and were sacred to the memory of five little brothers of mine –
who gave up trying to get a living,
exceedingly early in that universal struggle –
I am indebted for a belief I religiously entertained
that they had all been born on their backs
with their hands in their trousers-pockets,
and had never taken them out in this state of existence.

Ours was the marsh country,
down by the river,
within, as the river wound,
twenty miles of the sea.
My first most vivid and broad impression
of the identity of things,
seems to me to have

David Sudlow
b1980/UK
www.sudlowdesign.com

Margareta Ekarv is a Swedish writer whose
studies into adult literacy and comprehension
in the 1980s led her to develop new ways
of writing display texts for use in museums.
Ekarv recognised that museums can often
be noisy and distracting environments,
affecting a person's ability to concentrate and
take in new information. This informed her
guiding principles for writing and designing
museum texts, recognising the importance
of clarity of information, accessibility and
familiarity. She advocated that each line of
text should communicate only one idea,
that short lines make reading easier, that
texts should be consistent in length and
structured as a series of clauses. Once these
ideas are applied, the resulting text often
resembles a poem and is more organic in
structure than ranged left or justified setting.
Ekarv's was an integrated approach. She
believed that curating, writing, editing and
typographic design should not be handled
as separate tasks.

Glossary
counter
humanist sans serif

I have used Ekarv's theories to inform the design of my contribution to *Page 1* as I was interested to see the results when applied to this piece of prose. I chose the typeface National for all the text. The body text is set in Medium, 8.75/9.75pt and the title is set in Extra Bold, 10.75pt. Designed by Kris Sowersby, National is a clear, highly readable, humanist sans serif typeface with a wide range of alternative characters. The alternative lowercase 'a', 'g' and 'y' have been used. They have large counters and open-jaw designs that aid reading and accessibility.

Ekarv's techniques for writing have been adopted and adapted for use at the Royal Naval Museum, Portsmouth; the Egyptology gallery at Swansea Museum; and at the Churchill Museum, London.

National
Klim Type Foundry/Village
Kris Sowersby, 2007

Chapter heading
Extra Bold
10.75pt

Body text, folio
Medium
8.75/9.75pt

Sam Winston

Chapter I

My father's family name being Pirrip, and my christian name Philip, my infant tongue could make of both names nothing longer or more explicit than Pip. So, I called myself Pip, and came to be called Pip.

http://www.direct.gov.uk/en/DisabledPeople/HealthAndSupport/WhosWhoInHealthServices/DG_4003768
National Health Service - Speech and language therapists assess and treat children and adults who have difficulties with speech and language.

http://www.microsoft.com/typography/ctfonts/wordrecognition.aspx
Microsoft - The Science of Word Recognition

I give Pirrip as my father's family name, on the athority of his tombstone and my sister – Mrs. Joe Gargery, who married the blacksmith. As I never saw my father or my mother, and never saw any likeness of either of them (for their days were long before the days of photographs) my first fancies regarding what they were like, were unreasonably derived from their tombstones. The shape of the letters on my father's, gave me an odd idea that he was a square, stout, dark man, with curly black hair. From the character and turn of the inscription, "Also Georgiana Wife of the Above," I drew a childish conclusion that my mother was freckled and sickly. To five little stone lozenges, each about a foot and a half long, which were arranged in a neat row beside their grave, and were sacred to the memory of five little brothers of mine – who gave up trying to get a living, exceedingly early in that universal struggle – I am indebted for a belief I religiously entertained that they had all been born on their backs with their hands in their trousers-pockets, and had never taken them out in this state of existence.

http://www.nber.org/aginghealth/spring06/w11963.html
The Determinants of Mortality -Dramatic changes began in the 18th century, with life expectancy in England rising to 41 years

https://www.cia.gov/library/publications/the-world-factbook/fields/2102.html
Central Intelligance Agency - LIFE EXPECTANCY AT BIRTH 2011 Angola 38.76 years (est.)

Ours was the marsh country, down by the river, within, as the river wound, twenty miles of the sea. My first most vivid and broad impression of the identity of things, seems to me to have been gained on a memorable raw afternoon towards

Sam Winston
b1978/UK
www.samwinston.com

I initially read the page online so I chose
to set my contribution to *Page 1* in a way that
reflects changing reading habits.

The pencil lines trace where I hyperlinked
the text to websites that seemed relevant.
I wanted to reference this non-linear way
of reading that sees us constantly cross-
referencing and linking to other sources. My
Pip is now connected to the National Health
Service and his family deaths contextualised
by eighteenth-century mortality rates.

Instead of the normal 'depth' we experience
when reading a novel, as we are taken by
the author from the beginning through to
the end, we increasingly 'span' read – where
we surf across a vast amount of linked
information, sampled from multiple sources.
This is how a lot of our information is
now consumed.

Adobe Garamond Pro
Robert Slimbach, 1989
after Claude Garamond c1532
7/8.4pt

Winterhouse

Chapter One : Page One

MY FATHER'S FAMILY NAME BEING PIRRIP, and my christian name Philip, my infant tongue could make of both names nothing longer or more explicit than Pip. So, I called myself Pip, and came to be called Pip.

I give Pirrip as my father's family name, on the authority of his tombstone and my sister— Mrs. Joe Gargery, who married the blacksmith. As I never saw my father or my mother, and never saw any likeness of either of them (for their days were long before the days of photographs[1]), my first fancies regarding what they were like, were unreasonably derived from their tombstones. The shape of the letters[2] on my father's, gave me an odd idea that he was a square, stout, dark man, with curly black hair. From the character and turn of the inscription, *Also Georgiana Wife of the Above,* I drew a childish conclusion that my mother was freckled and sickly. To five little stone lozenges,[3] each about a foot and a half long, which were arranged in a neat row beside their grave, and were sacred to the memory of five little brothers of mine—who gave up trying to get a living, exceedingly early in that universal struggle—I am indebted for a belief I religiously entertained that they had all been born on their backs with their hands in their trousers-pockets[4], and had never taken them out in this state of existence.

Ours was the marsh country, down by the river, within, as the river wound, twenty miles of the sea. My first most vivid and broad impression of the identity of things, seems to me to have

NOTES.

[1] *The first real photograph was produced in 1826 by the French inventor Joseph Nicéphore Niépce.*

CLARENDON EXTENDED.

[2] *Clarendon is an English slab-serif typeface designed by Robert Besley for the Fann Street Foundry in 1845.*

[3] *The "stone lozenges" (above) were probably inspired by the churchyard graves in the town of Cooling, in Kent.*

[4] *The author's nod to 'pockets' may well foreshadow the introduction of the Pocket family—Herbert, Matthew and Sarah—who become important in Pip's story.*

Winterhouse
www.winterhouse.com

Jessica Helfand
b1960/USA

William Drenttel
b1953/USA

Our approach was to visually, verbally and contextually deconstruct the page and to probe a number of elements *within* the text that could be annotated.

It was the mention of 'trousers-pockets' that led us to our friend Hannah Carlson, who is writing her dissertation on the history of the pocket itself. Carlson writes:

The admonition to 'take your hands out of your pockets, young man!' was a staple of etiquette manuals in the eighteenth and nineteenth centuries ... a gesture coded by social critics as one of the 'bad habits peculiar to boys' [1] *(as only boys and men had trouser pockets). It was considered a 'vulgar' and 'uncouth' gesture because of its ties to the body – its too-frank acknowledgement of the body (some expensive public schools in Britain sewed up boys' trouser pockets to help train their charges). But the gesture was also a sign of laziness and inactivity – a rebuke to the striving, ambitious, self-perfecting tendencies of the middle class (and perhaps of the adult world).*

Indeed, Dickens himself, Carlson told us, associated the loafer (a figure often depicted with his hands in his pockets) with the down-and-out:

In his American Notes, *he complained of the 'two or three half-drunken loafers [who] come loitering out with their hands in their pockets' during stage-coach changes.* [2] *Boys were warned against loaferism. 'Who would be a loafer?' asked a front-page editorial appearing in the December 1853 issue of* The Youth's Companion. *'Just look at the picture! See what lazy, ragged, good-for-nothing sorts of fellows they are!'*

[1]
Cornelia Holroyd and Bradley Richards,
At Home and Abroad,
Evans and Brittan, 1858,
p40.

[2]
Charles Dickens,
American Notes,
Appleton and Co, 1868
[1842], p79.

Hoefler Text
Roman, Italic and Small Caps
Hoefler & Frere-Jones
Jonathan Hoefler, 1991

Workshop

Workshop
www.letterpressworkshop.com

Alexander Cooper
b1973/UK

Rose Gridneff
b1983/UK

Great Expectations was originally published between 1860 and 1861 in the weekly publication *All The Year Round*, a literary journal owned by Charles Dickens.

The novel's transition from magazine to book was not a straightforward one. The first edition, published in July 1861, had poor sales as its main readership had already read it in its serialised form. The publishers, Chapman & Hall, decided to address this by 'tipping in' additional title pages that stated these books were new editions, despite being from the same print run. By the end of 1861 at least five of these 'editions' had been published.

This page explores the change in form between the ephemera of a publication and the permanence of a book, exploring how reader expectations change depending upon format, and how it alters the way the text is read. The structure and layout from *All The Year Round* is replicated, while using only the copy from *Page 1*. It is printed on a separate sheet to highlight these differences and echo the tipped in pages from the earlier editions.

Modern No 20
Roman and Italic
Stephenson Blake, 1905
10pt set solid

Charlie Borley

MY FATHER'S
FAMILY NAME BEING

PIRRIP,

AND MY CHRISTIAN NAME PHILIP, MY INFANT TONGUE COULD
MAKE OF BOTH NAMES NOTHING LONGER OR MORE EXPLICIT THAN
PIP. SO, I CALLED MYSELF PIP, AND CAME TO BE CALLED PIP.

I GIVE PIRRIP AS MY FATHER'S FAMILY NAME, ON THE AUTHORITY OF HIS TOMBSTONE AND MY
SISTER – MRS. JOE GARGERY, WHO MARRIED THE BLACKSMITH. AS I NEVER SAW MY FATHER OR
MY MOTHER, AND NEVER SAW ANY LIKENESS OF EITHER OF THEM (FOR THEIR DAYS WERE LONG
BEFORE THE DAYS OF PHOTOGRAPHS), MY FIRST FANCIES REGARDING WHAT THEY WERE LIKE,
WERE UNREASONABLY DERIVED FROM THEIR TOMBSTONES. THE SHAPE OF THE LETTERS ON MY
FATHER'S, GAVE ME AN ODD IDEA THAT HE WAS A SQUARE, STOUT, DARK MAN, WITH CURLY BLACK
HAIR. FROM THE CHARACTER AND TURN OF THE INSCRIPTION,

"ALSO

GEORGIANA

WIFE OF THE ABOVE,"

I DREW A CHILDISH CONCLUSION THAT MY MOTHER WAS FRECKLED AND SICKLY. TO FIVE LITTLE
STONE LOZENGES, EACH ABOUT A FOOT AND A HALF LONG, WHICH WERE ARRANGED IN A NEAT
ROW BESIDE THEIR GRAVE, AND WERE SACRED TO THE MEMORY OF FIVE LITTLE BROTHERS OF MINE
– WHO GAVE UP TRYING TO GET A LIVING, EXCEEDINGLY EARLY IN THAT UNIVERSAL STRUGGLE –
I AM INDEBTED FOR A BELIEF I RELIGIOUSLY ENTERTAINED THAT THEY HAD ALL BEEN BORN ON
THEIR BACKS WITH THEIR HANDS IN THEIR TROUSERS-POCKETS, AND HAD NEVER TAKEN THEM OUT
IN THIS STATE OF EXISTENCE.

OURS WAS THE MARSH COUNTRY, DOWN BY THE RIVER,
WITHIN, AS THE RIVER WOUND, TWENTY MILES OF THE
SEA. MY FIRST MOST VIVID AND BROAD IMPRESSION OF
THE IDENTITY OF THINGS, SEEMS TO ME TO HAVE

PAGE ONE

Charlie Borley
b1990/UK
www.charlieborley.co.uk

BA Graphic Design student
Kingston University, London
UK

In my *Page 1* design I wanted to mimic
the layout and style of a headstone because
Pip's recollection and description of his
parents is based upon the inscriptions
on their gravestone. I hand-rendered the
lettering as I thought the imperfections
not dissimilar to those found on manually-
engraved inscriptions. The texture and
smudging humanises the design. I have
used variation in lettering size, not only for
aesthetic reasons but also to emphasise
names and some passages of the text.
It also allows the reader to skim read the
text. Mine is perhaps a morbid approach,
but I think it sets the appropriate tone.

lettering based on

Baskerville Old Face
Isaac Moore, 1768

Franklin Gothic Book
Morris Fuller Benton, 1904
Victor Caruso, 1980

Daniel Eatock

CHAPTER 1

My father's family name being Pirrip, and my christian name Philip, my infant tongue could make of both names nothing longer or more explicit than Pip. So, I called myself Pip, and came to be called Pip.

I give Pirrip as my father's family name, on the authority of his tombstone and my sister – Mrs. Joe Gargery, who married the blacksmith. As I never saw my father or my mother, and never saw any likeness of either of them (for their days were long before the days of photographs), my first fancies regarding what they were like, were unreasonably derived from their tombstones. The shape of the letters on my father's, gave me an odd idea that he was a square, stout, dark man, with curly black hair. From the character and turn of the inscription, "*Also Georgiana Wife of the Above*," I drew a childish conclusion that my mother was freckled and sickly. To five little stone lozenges, each about a foot and a half long, which were arranged in a neat row beside their grave, and were sacred to the memory of five little brothers of mine – who gave up trying to get a living, exceedingly early in that universal struggle – I am indebted for a belief I religiously entertained that they had all been born on their backs with their hands in their trousers-pockets, and had never taken them out in this state of existence.

Ours was the marsh country, down by the river, within, as the river wound, twenty miles of the sea. My first most vivid and broad impression of the identity of things, seems to me to have

1

Daniel Eatock
b1975/UK
www.eatock.com

The image in the brief [1] shows the text in
a format that is perfectly legible – I choose to
use this formatting as a given/ready-made.

[1]
The brief showed page 1
of *Great Expectations*
by Charles Dickens,
Collins Classics, Harper
Press, an imprint of
HarperCollinsPublishers,
2010 edition.

as the Collins Classics edition, 2010
Kalix
Regular and Italic
Linotype
Franko Luin, 1994
8/9.8pt

Fraser Muggeridge studio

Fraser Muggeridge studio
www.pleasedonotbend.co.uk
www.typographysummerschool.org

Fraser Muggeridge
b1973/UK

Images, images and more images.
People love images.
The image is king.
Text is over.
Rest in peace.

Our alphabet, as we know it, was derived
indirectly from pictures that became
symbols, which became letters, which
we join together to form words and
sentences. To read and to imagine,
that's what we learn at school.

Let's forget text and just use images, it will
be much more fun. Join me for the revolution.
We will just use images as text. Let's give
it a go.

Does it work?

Um, not really.

Actually not at all.

Well it was worth a

karlssonwilker inc

karlssonwilker inc
www.karlssonwilker.com

Piera Wolf
b1983/Switzerland

We wanted to create something amazing,
so we gave it an award.

Sam Piyasena, aka Billie Jean

My father's family name being Pirrip, and my christian name Philip, my infant tongue could make of both names nothing longer or more explicit than Pip. So, I called myself Pip, and came to be called Pip. I give Pirrip as my father's family name, on the authority of his tombstone and my sister – Mrs. Joe Gargery, who married the blacksmith. As I never saw my father or my mother, and never saw any likeness of either of them (for their days were long before the days of photographs), my first fancies regarding what they were like, were unreasonably derived from their tombstones. The shape of the letters on my father's, gave me an odd idea that he was a square, stout, dark man, with curly black hair. From the character and turn of the inscription, "Also Georgiana Wife of the Above," I drew a childish conclusion that my mother was freckled and sickly. To five little stone lozenges, each about a foot and a half long, which were arranged in a neat row beside their grave, and were sacred to the memory of five little brothers of mine – who gave up trying to get a living, exceedingly early in that universal struggle – I am indebted for a belief I religiously entertained that they had all been born on their backs with their hands in their trousers-pockets, and had never taken them out in this state of existence. Ours was the marsh country, down by the river, within, as the river wound, twenty miles of the sea. My first most vivid and broad impression of the identity of things, seems to me to have

Sam Piyasena, aka Billie Jean
b1965/UK
www.billiejean.co.uk

My first encounter with Dickens was as
a young boy in the early 1970s. My mum took
me to a screening of the film version of Lionel
Bart's *Oliver*. I loved it, and still do to this day.
My next encounter with Dickens came a few
years later in my local library with a dusty
old large-print edition of *Great Expectations*.
I didn't have poor eyesight, but the large 16pt
type was like a comfort blanket and certainly
made the prospect of rading the novel
less daunting. From then on, I was hooked.
Hooked on Dickens and on reading.

My schoolboy concerns about legibility
have been cut adrift for this piece. I'm an
illustrator, not a typographer, and so wanted
to make a picture of my design for *Page 1*.

Shadows loom large in *Great Expectations*.
Pip's encounters with Magwitch, Estella
and Miss Havisham are continually cloaked
in shadowy misunderstandings. There are
foreboding shadows throughout the plot,
which only eventually clear when the light
of revelation is cast upon them.

In my local public library, it is reassuring
to see that *Great Expectations* still has
a presence in a variety of formats (from audio
book to large print!). However, it is troubling
to know that this particular library is under
threat of closure. Harrow Green Library is
situated in one of the most deprived parts
of east London and recent public spending
cuts have been disastrous for this area.
The ever-growing disparity between the rich
and poor has echoes of Dickensian London.
His nineteenth-century themes still resonate
today and ensure that his work is relevant
to a twenty-first-century audience.

lettering based on
Georgia
Matthew Carter, 1996

Studio Frith

MY FATHER'S FAMILY NAME BEING PIRRIP, AND MY CHRISTIAN NAME PHILIP, MY INFANT TONGUE COULD MAKE OF BOTH NAMES NOTHING LONGER OR MORE EXPLICIT THAN PIP. SO, I CALLED MYSELF PIP, AND CAME TO BE CALLED PIP. I GIVE PIRRIP AS MY FATHER'S FAMILY NAME, ON THE AUTHORITY OF HIS TOMBSTONE AND MY SISTER — MRS. JOE GARGERY, WHO MARRIED THE BLACKSMITH. AS I NEVER SAW MY FATHER OR MY MOTHER, AND NEVER SAW ANY LIKENESS OF EITHER OF THEM (FOR THEIR DAYS WERE LONG BEFORE THE DAYS OF PHOTOGRAPHS), MY FIRST FANCIES REGARDING WHAT THEY WERE LIKE, WERE UNREASONABLY DERIVED FROM THEIR TOMBSTONES. THE SHAPE OF THE LETTERS ON MY FATHER'S, GAVE ME AN ODD IDEA THAT HE WAS A SQUARE, STOUT, DARK MAN, WITH CURLY BLACK HAIR. FROM THE CHARACTER AND TURN OF THE INSCRIPTION, "ALSO GEORGIANA WIFE OF THE ABOVE," I DREW A CHILDISH CONCLUSION THAT MY MOTHER WAS FRECKLED AND SICKLY. TO FIVE LITTLE STONE LOZENGES, EACH ABOUT A FOOT AND A HALF LONG, WHICH WERE ARRANGED IN A NEAT ROW BESIDE THEIR GRAVE, AND WERE SACRED TO THE MEMORY OF FIVE LITTLE BROTHERS OF MINE — WHO GAVE UP TRYING TO GET A LIVING, EXCEEDINGLY EARLY IN THAT UNIVERSAL STRUGGLE — I AM INDEBTED FOR A BELIEF I RELIGIOUSLY ENTERTAINED THAT THEY HAD ALL BEEN BORN ON THEIR BACKS WITH THEIR HANDS IN THEIR TROUSERS-POCKETS, AND HAD NEVER TAKEN THEM OUT IN THIS STATE OF EXISTENCE. OURS WAS THE MARSH COUNTRY, DOWN BY THE RIVER, WITHIN, AS THE RIVER WOUND, TWENTY MILES OF THE SEA. MY FIRST MOST VIVID AND BROAD IMPRESSION OF THE IDENTITY OF THINGS, SEEMS TO ME TO HAVE

Studio Frith
www.studiofrith.com

The motif of lock and key runs throughout
Great Expectations, in the book's descriptions
of criminality and confinement along
with detailed passages about Victorian
prisons. Our design for *Page 1* is set as
a concrete poem in the form of a Victorian
key bow.

In keeping with the period in which Dickens
was writing, we have used a Grotesque
typeface as this style of sans serif originated
in the nineteenth century.

Glossary
Grotesque [type]
sans serif

Monotype Grotesque
Frank Pierpont, 1926

James Ward

My father's family name being Pirrip, and my christian name Philip, my infant tongue could make of both names nothing longer or more explicit than Pip. So, I called myself Pip, and came to be called Pip. I give Pirrip as my father's family name, on the authority of his tombstone and my sister - Mrs. Joe Gargery, who married the blacksmith. As I never saw my father or my mother, and never saw any likeness of either of them (for their days were long before the days of photographs), my first fancies regarding what they were like, were unreasonably derived from their tombstones. The shape of the letters on my father's, gave me an odd idea that he was a square, stout, dark man, with curly black hair. From the character and turn of the inscription, "Also Georgiana Wife of the Above," I drew a childish conclusion that my mother was freckled and sickly. To five little stone lozenges, each about a foot and a half long, which were arranged in a neat row beside their grave, and were sacred to the memory of five little brothers of mine - who gave up trying to get a living, exceedingly early in that universal struggle - I am indebted for a belief I religiously entertained that they had all been born on their backs with their hands in their trousers-pockets, and had never taken them out in this state of existence. Ours was the marsh country, down by the river, within, as the river wound, twenty miles of the sea. My first most vivid and broad impression of the identity of things, seems to me to have

James Ward
b1989/UK
www.james-ward.co.uk

BA Graphic Design student
Kingston University, London
UK

I decided to lay out my contribution to
Page 1 in the shape of a moustache.

Pip is aspiring to lead a different way of life
and his 'great expectation' is to become a
gentleman. In the 1860s, when the book was
first published, a finely-shaped moustache
was both fashionable and commonplace for
many gentlemen.

My typographic moustache is positioned
on the page where the mouth might be if
the page were a face. I like the way that the
distinctive swash on the uppercase Old Face
'Q' mimics the curved tapered shape of
the moustache.

Glossary
Old Face [type]
swash [character]

Baskerville Old Face Regular
Isaac Moore, 1768

Body text
(moustache)
3.32pt

Chapter heading, folio
7pt

B.C...A.D.

Chapter I.

My father's family name being Pirrip, and my Christian name Philip, my infant tongue could make of both names nothing longer or more explicit than **PIP**. So, I called myself **PIP**, and came to be called **PIP**.

I give Pirrip as my father's family name, on the authority of his tombstone and my sister—Mrs. Joe Gargery, who married the blacksmith. As I never saw my father or my mother, and never saw any likeness of either of them (for their days were long before the days of photographs), my first fancies regarding what they were like, were unreasonably derived from their tombstones. The shape of the letters on my father's, gave me an odd idea that he was a square, stout, dark man, with curly black hair. From the character and turn of the inscription,

ALSO GEORGIANA
WIFE OF THE ABOVE   ,

I drew a childish conclusion that my mother was freckled and sickly. To five little stone lozenges, each about a foot and a half long, which were arranged in a neat row beside their grave, and were sacred to the memory of five little brothers of mine—who gave up trying to get a living, exceedingly early in that universal struggle—I am indebted for a belief

B.C...A.D.
www.benjamincritton.com

Benjamin Critton
b1983/USA

The type in this design for *Page 1* is set in 10pt and 32pt. The setting uses Larish Alte (drawn between 2006–11 by Radim Peško) and an alternate cut of Haas Unica Medium, initially drawn by André Gürtler, Christian Mengelt and Erich Gschwind and amended over the course of 2010–11 for use in a book called *The Etiquette in Connecticut*.

Both of these typefaces have stylistic alternatives so that, quite literally, the same character can be rendered in several ways, appearing in one form or another at different moments in a text. In this narrative Dickens' protagonist is mutable, behaving differently at any given moment in accordance with the company he keeps. Curiously, a double-storey 'a' feels vaguely more mannered than the single-storey equivalent character; gentleman Pip as opposed to blacksmith Pip, perhaps.

These typefaces seek audience. They are not humble, either in weight or character, which in a way speaks as much to Pip's id and ego as it does to this designer's; the expectations they have are, indeed, great.

Glossary
cut [as in type]
double-storey [character]
grid
gutter
single-storey [character]

They seemingly hope to hark back to another time while simultaneously being contemporary. These typefaces want to be relevant in ever-new contexts, as Dickens' work so effortlessly is (Ethan Hawke as Finn [Pip], the New York painter, circa 1998 in Alfonso Cuarón's film version; a former girlfriend exclaiming, in 2011, that she *totally* identifies with Estella).

Other facets of the composition include the elevation of the protagonist's name 'PIP', set always in capitals, and the formal emphasising of the grave inscription, which we find Pip analysing at the start of the narrative.

In addition, the faux-Tschicholdian grid employs the margins of a left-hand page despite this page falling on the right, leaving ample room for the gutter (from which Pip could be said to have crawled), as well as a vast space at the bottom of the page for an obnoxiously large folio: page 1.

Display type, folio
Haas Unica Medium
Haas Type Foundry
Erich Gschwind,
André Gürtler,
Christian Mengelt, 1980
redrawn
Benjamin Critton, 2010–11

Body text
Larish Alte Semibold
RP
10/11.5pt
Radim Peško, 2006–11

Colophon

Chapter I

My father's family name being Pirrip, and my christian name Philip, my infant tongue could make of both names nothing longer or more explicit than Pip. So, I called myself Pip, and came to be called Pip.

I give Pirrip as my father's family name, on the authority of his tombstone and my sister ~ Mrs. Joe Gargery, who married the blacksmith. As I never saw my father or my mother, and never saw any likeness of either of them (for their days were long before the days of photographs), my first fancies regarding what they were like, were unreasonably derived from their tombstones. The shape of the letters on my father's, gave me an odd idea that he was a square, stout, dark man, with curly black hair. From the character and turn of the inscription, "Also Georgiana Wife of the Above," I drew a childish conclusion that my mother was freckled and sickly. To five little stone lozenges, each about a foot and a half long, which were arranged in a neat row beside their grave, and were sacred to the memory of five little brothers of mine ~ who gave up trying to get a living, exceedingly early in that universal struggle ~ I am indebted for a belief I religiously entertained that they had all been born on their backs with their hands in their trousers-pockets, and had never taken them out in this state of existence.

Ours was the marsh country, down by the river, within, as the river wound, twenty miles of the sea. My first most vivid and broad impression of the identity of things, seems to me to have been gained on a

1

Colophon
www.colophon.info

David Bennewith
b1977/New Zealand

The motivation for this contribution to
Page 1 comes from an essay by British writer
and artist Paul Elliman about Samoan-born,
New Zealand-based typographer Joseph
Churchward. Elliman looks more closely at
the typeface Māori designed by Churchward.
Its letterforms reference the shape of fern
furls, and in his essay Elliman contemplates
the relationship between this lettering
and aspects inherent to the process
of colonialism:

*Typography, as the incarnate spirit of an
industrialised world, can seem so much a part
of the 'fabric' of imperialist culture and its
sense of both moral and material superiority.
Yet here, in the Maori font, the imperial order
of the word collides with the forms and
accents of a subaltern Polynesian culture.
As a further example of 'the empire writing
back',* [1] *the territorial expansion that was
driven by a need to acquire raw materials is
countered in the letterforms by an inscribed
reference to the land itself.* [2]

In my layout for *Page 1*, I used my digitised version of Churchward's Māori to express Pip's encounter with the 'most vivid and broad impression of the identity of things'. My intention was to put some ideas inherent in Elliman's essay into practice. In particular, the suggestion that a typeface could 'decide, at any moment, to become unintelligible, or simply uncooperative' and that a writing system could 'suddenly reconcile its language to the inscrutable force of the land'. [3]

While going through the process of tracing the Māori letterforms I became interested in the total absence of straight lines and repeated motifs, which are usually present in a typeface design. This challenges an implied logic of the designed and digitised alphabet; possibly in favour of more intuitive, intrinsic and rebellious notions applied to what is usually considered a closed and hermetic system.

[1]
A reference to a publication considered a 'seminal intervention in the field of post-colonial studies'. *The Empire Writes Back: Theory and Practice in Post-colonial Literatures* Bill Ashcroft, Gareth Griffiths and Helen Triffin New Accents, 2002.

[2]
'And Joseph Churchward' by Paul Elliman in *Joseph Churchward* [Churchward International Typefaces]. Editor David Bennewith Jan van Eyck Academie, Clouds and Colophon, 2009, p252.

[3]
ibid, p248.

Churchward Māori Regular
Churchward International Typefaces
Joseph Churchward, 1985
digitisation Colophon.info, 2011
11/11.5pt

Fitzroy & Finn

CHAPTER 1

MY FATHERS FAMILY NAME BEING PIRRIP AND MY CHRISTIAN NAME PHILIP MY INFANT TONGUE COULD MAKE OF BOTH NAMES NOTHING LONGER OR MORE EXPLICIT THAN PIP SO I CALLED MYSELF PIP AND CAME TO BE CALLED PIP I GIVE PIRRIP AS MY FATHERS FAMILY NAME ON THE AUTHORITY OF HIS TOMBSTONE AND MY SISTER MRS JOE GARGERY WHO MARRIED THE BLACKSMITH AS I NEVER SAW MY FATHER OR MY MOTHER AND NEVER SAW ANY LIKENESS OF EITHER OF THEM FOR THEIR DAYS WERE LONG BEFORE THE DAYS OF PHOTOGRAPHS MY FIRST FANCIES REGARDING WHAT THEY WERE LIKE WERE UNREASONABLY DERIVED FROM THEIR TOMBSTONES THE SHAPE OF THE LETTERS ON MY FATHERS GAVE ME AN ODD IDEA THAT HE WAS A SQUARE STOUT DARK MAN WITH CURLY BLACK HAIR FROM THE CHARACTER AND TURN OF THE INSCRIPTION ALSO GEORGIANA WIFE OF THE ABOVE I DREW A CHILDISH CONCLUSION THAT MY MOTHER WAS FRECKLED AND SICKLY TO FIVE LITTLE STONE LOZENGES EACH ABOUT A FOOT AND A HALF LONG WHICH WERE ARRANGED IN A NEAT ROW BESIDE THEIR GRAVE AND WERE SACRED TO THE MEMORY OF FIVE LITTLE BROTHERS OF MINE WHO GAVE UP TRYING TO GET A LIVING EXCEEDINGLY EARLY IN THAT UNIVERSAL STRUGGLE I AM INDEBTED FOR A BELIEF I RELIGIOUSLY ENTERTAINED THAT THEY HAD ALL BEEN BORN ON THEIR BACKS WITH THEIR HANDS IN THEIR TROUSERS POCKETS AND HAD NEVER TAKEN THEM OUT IN THIS STATE OF EXISTENCE OURS WAS THE MARSH COUNTRY DOWN BY THE RIVER WITHIN AS THE RIVER WOUND TWENTY MILES OF THE SEA MY FIRST MOST VIVID AND BROAD IMPRESSION OF THE IDENTITY OF THINGS SEEMS TO ME TO HAVE

Fitzroy & Finn
www.fitzroyandfinn.co.uk

Paul Finn
b1977/UK

When I first read the text I was particularly drawn to this passage '...five little stone lozenges, each about a foot and a half long, which were arranged in a neat row beside their grave'. This prompted me to arrange my contribution to *Page 1* in five columns, and in so doing reference the rows of graves in a cemetery. Centred type reinforced this relationship. The words look like the names of the departed on a monument to the dead. Removing all the punctuation reinforced this idea further.

The typeface is Martin Majoor's robust and elegant Nexus Sans Bold, with the five columns set in 6pt small caps, which seemed fitting in feel for those who have passed away.

FF Nexus Sans Bold
FontFont
Martin Majoor, 2004

Kate Jones

CHAPTER I

My father's family name being Pirrip, and my christian name Philip, my infant tongue could make of both names nothing longer or more explicit than Pip. So, I called myself Pip, and came to be called Pip.

I give Pirrip as my father's family name, on the authority of his tombstone and my sister – Mrs. Joe Gargery, who married the blacksmith. As I never saw my father or my mother, and never saw any likeness of either of them (for their days were long before the days of photographs), my first fancies regarding what they were like, were unreasonably derived from their tombstones. The shape of the letters on my father's, gave me an odd idea that he was a square, stout, dark man, with curly black hair. From the character and turn of the inscription, "Also Georgiana Wife of the Above," I drew a childish conclusion that my mother was freckled and sickly. To five little stone lozenges, each about a foot and a half long, which were arranged in a neat row beside their grave, and were sacred to the memory of five little brothers of mine – who gave up trying to get a living, exceedingly early in that universal struggle – I am indebted for a belief I religiously entertained that they had all been born on their backs with their hands in their trousers-pockets, and had never taken them out in this state of existence.

Ours was the marsh country, down by the river, within, as the river wound, twenty miles of the sea. My first most vivid and broad impression of the identity of things, seems to me to have

Kate Jones
b1990/UK
www.kate-j.co.uk

BA Graphic Design student
University of Brighton
UK

When setting the type for my *Page 1* design,
I wanted to represent the fluctuating
emotional journey of Pip that is told in
the novel.

I have used uneven kerning to mimic
the uneasy periods in Pip's life and have
therefore used a narrow text measure to help
read what is, in parts, a challenging layout.
I have used the typeface Bookman Old Style,
which was designed in the same decade as
Great Expectations was first published and is
relatively easy to read when either tightly
kerned or more generously spaced.

Glossary
kerning

Body text
Bookman Old Style Regular
Monotype
American Type Founders
Bruce Type Foundry
Alexander Phemister, 1860
7/12pt

Cecilia Lindgren

Chapter 1

My father's family name being Pirrip, and my christian name Philip, my infant tongue could make of both names nothing longer or more explicit than Pip. So, I called myself Pip, and came to be called ▬

▬ I give Pirrip as my father's family name, on the authority of his tombstone and my sister – Mrs. Joe Gargery, who married the blacksmith. As I never saw my father or my mother, and never saw any likeness of either of them (for their days were long before the days of photographs), my first fancies regarding what they were like, were unreasonably derived from their tombstones. The shape of the letters on my father's, gave me an odd idea that he was a square, stout, dark man, with curly black hair. From the character and turn of the inscription, "Also Georgiana Wife of the Above," I drew a childish conclusion that my mother was freckled and sickly. To five little stone lozenges, each about a foot and a half long, which were arranged in a neat row beside their grave, and were sacred to the memory of five little brothers of mine – who gave up trying to get a living, exceedingly early in that universal struggle – I am indebted for a belief I religiously entertained that they had all been born on their backs with their hands in their trousers-pockets, and had never taken them out in this state of existence.

▬ Ours was the marsh country, down by the river, within, as the river wound, twenty miles of the sea. My first most vivid and broad impression of the identity of things, seems to me to have

Cecilia Lindgren
b1978/Sweden
www.cecilialindgren.com

I decided to typeset my design for *Page 1* in Perpetua (designed by Eric Gill in 1928), mainly because of its inscriptional quality. I wanted the type to echo the setting of the novel's opening scene, where the main character, Pip, is surrounded by headstones in a graveyard. The framing of the page references the language of tombstones as well as classical book design, with the outer frame using the same proportions as the actual page.

Though not designed at the same time as *Great Expectations* was first published, The typeface Perpetua has some of the same characteristics as the fonts of that period. It can be classified as a Transitional typeface because of its contrasting thick and thin strokes and bracketed serifs. This typographic classification could (perhaps in a slightly far-fetched way) also reference the idea of Pip's development and transition throughout the book.

As Pip is the protagonist of the novel and introduced on the opening page, I thought it would be interesting to highlight his name rather than use a traditional drop cap as the typographic focal point. This also gives the setting a modern twist.

Glossary
drop capital
serif
Transitional [type]

Body text
Perpetua
Monotype
Eric Gill, 1928
9.5/11pt

Peter Nencini

CHAPTER 1

My father's family name being Pirrip, and my christian name Philip, my infant tongue could make of both names nothing longer or more explicit than Pip. So, I called myself Pip, and came to be called Pip.

I give Pirrip as my father's family name, on the authority of his tombstone and my sister – Mrs. Joe Gargery, who married the blacksmith. As I never saw my father or my mother, and never saw any likeness of either of them (for their days were long before the days of photographs), my first fancies regarding what they were like, were unreasonably derived from their tombstones. The shape of the letters on my father's, gave me an odd idea that he was a square, stout, dark man, with curly black hair. From the character and turn of the inscription, "Also Georgiana Wife of the Above," I drew a childish conclusion that my mother was freckled and sickly. To five little stone lozenges, each about a foot and a half long, which were arranged in a neat row beside their grave, and were sacred to the memory of five little brothers of mine – who gave up trying to get a living, exceedingly early in that universal struggle – I am indebted for a belief I religiously entertained that they had all been born on their backs with their hands in their trousers-pockets, and had never taken them out in this state of existence.

Ours was the marsh country, down by the river, within, as the river wound, twenty miles of the sea. My first most vivid and broad impression of the identity of things, seems to me to have

1

Peter Nencini
b1968/UK
www.peternencini.co.uk
www.peternencini.blogspot.com

I am calling my *Page 1* design 'Faces, Ornaments and Gaucheries'. It uses three new variants of my font Make Do, a family of monoline, monospaced characters with clunky, limited attributes. Make Do is a typeface derived from experiments in drawing, and memory of type before one knows anything of what typography is. It stems from combining remembered traces of both handwriting exercises as a child and the highly geometric forms of Paul Renner's font Futura.

Each of the three variants in this layout is used to emphasise different parts of the text. Two of the three variants use a calligraphic stroke, referencing the mid-nineteenth-century revival of Caslon and Old Faces more generally. As a left-hander it is obvious to me from the inflections of the character strokes in these original fonts that they were cut by right-handed people. So, I have developed the notion of a gaucherie – drawing a counterpointed 'left-handed' stroke that I have added to some characters. It quietly leans the wrong way, its 'leftness' giving itself away as Make Do Gauche in a sentence of Make Do Droite. Another variant, Make Do Great Primer, based on the nineteenth-century sans serif, is used for facts and names.

Glossary
cut [as in type]
Old Face [type]
sans serif

▬▬▬▬▬▬▬▬▬▬▬▬▬▬▬▬▬▬▬▬▬

Finally, I have included ornamentation
to add a sense of aspiration, influenced by
motorhome livery graphics, which carry
a nondescript message of on-the-road
betterment and a punch-the-air shoe as
'cursor' to mark the copy cut-off, and
the rite of passage to come.

▬▬▬▬▬▬▬▬▬▬▬▬▬▬▬▬▬▬▬▬▬

Make Do
Peter Nencini, 2009–12
8.5/11.5pt

Quentin B.

Chapter
I

My father's family name being *Pirrip*, and my christian name
Philip, my infant tongue *could make* of both names nothing
longer or more explicit than *Pip*. So, I called myself *Pip*, and
came to be called Pip.

I give Pirrip as my father's family name, on *the* authority
of his tombstone and my sister – *Mrs.* Joe Gargery, *who* married
the *blacksmith*. As I never saw my *father* or my mother, and
never *saw any* likeness of either of them *(for their* days were long
before the *days* of photographs), *my first fancies regarding* what
they were like, were unreasonably derived from their
tombstones. The *shape* of *the letters* on my father's, gave me an
odd idea *that he was a* square, *stout, dark* man, with curly black
hair. From *the* character and turn of the inscription, "Also
Georgiana *Wife* of *the Above*," I drew a childish conclusion that
my *mother* was freckled and *sickly.* To five little stone lozenges,
each about a foot and a half long, which *were arranged* in a neat
row beside their *grave*, and *were sacred to the memory* of five
little brothers of mine – *who gave up trying to* get a living,
exceedingly early in that universal struggle – *I am* indebted for
a belief I *religiously entertained* that they had all been born on
their backs with *their hands in their* trousers-pockets, and had
never taken them out *in this state* of existence.

Ours was the marsh country, down *by the river*, within, as
the river wound, twenty miles of *the* sea. *My first most vivid* and
broad impression of the identity of things, seems to me to have

Quentin B.
www.quentinb.fr

Quentin Berthelot
b1988/France

In my design for *Page 1*, I wanted to visually recreate Pip's emotions when he sees his family's gravestones. My main intention was to graphically express and display these feelings to engender empathy in the reader.

The first lines of *Great Expectations* introduce Pip's curiosity about who he is, and the reader becomes immediately aware that he is searching for clues about his family and his personal history. To me, he appears disoriented, almost fumbling in the dark. By distorting the text, so that it appears to be tactile and three-dimensional in parts, it might be said to visually evoke the representation of a face as felt by the hands of a blind man. In doing so, the reading experience is changed. The distortion places the reader in the same situation as a child, forced to read carefully to capture all the details of the text. The minimalism of the layout highlights this effect. The font is Lydian MT, which I chose as it is reminiscent of calligraphy.

Lydian MT Regular
Monotype
Warren Chappell, 1938
9.75pt

Leonardo Sonnoli

Chapter I

My father's
family name being **PIRRIP** ,

and my christian name **PHILIP** ,

my infant tongue could
make of both names
nothing longer or more
explicit than **PIP** .

So, I called myself **PIP** ,

and came
to be called **PIP**

I give **PIRRIP**

as my father's family name,
on the authority of his
tombstone and my sister – **MRS JOE GARGERY**

who married the blacksmith. As I never saw my father or my mother, and
never saw any likeness of either of them (for their days were long before the
days of photographs), my first fancies regarding what they were like, were unreasonably derived from their tombstones. The shape of the letters on my
father's, gave me an odd idea that he was a square, stout, dark man, with curly black hair. From the character and turn of the inscription,

"Also **GEORGIANA** *Wife of the Above,"*
I drew a childish conclusion that my mother was freckled and sickly. To five
little stone lozenges, each about a foot and a half long, which were arranged
in a neat row beside their grave, and were sacred to the memory of five little
brothers of mine – who gave up trying to get a living, exceedingly early in that
universal struggle – I am indebted for a belief I religiously entertained that
they had all been born on their backs with their hands in their trousers-pockets, and had never taken them out in this state of existence.

Ours was the marsh country, down by the river, within, as the
river wound, twenty miles of the sea. My first most vivid and
broad impression of the identity of things, seems to me to have

Leonardo Sonnoli
b1962/Italy
www.sonnoli.com

What is 'Dickensian' today? Can Dickens' novels tell us about our world and not just a Victorian one? These questions were the starting point for my attempt to visualise and typographically represent the world of those who are weak and outcast from contemporary Western society – those who seek to be heard and dream of a better life.

Nowadays, in the Dickensian suburbs, young graffiti artists express themselves in and out of the ghetto by tagging public surfaces with a mark or name. Behind these tags there are often very tough stories that rarely come out, there are many young Pips with great expectations.

In this first page of the novel Pip visualises his father and mother through his interpretation of typographic characters. My 'calligraphic' equivalents harness the anger of the weakest people to deface a bourgeois and reactionary 8pt Baskerville page 1.

Monotype Baskerville
Monotype Type Drawing Office, 1923
after John Baskerville, c1757

Chapter heading
Semibold
10pt

Body text
Regular and Italic
8/9pt

Sueh Li Tan

CHAPTER 1

MY FATHER'S FAMILY NAME BEING PIRRIP, AND MY CHRISTIAN NAME PHILIP, MY INFANT TONGUE COULD MAKE OF BOTH NAMES NOTHING LONGER OR MORE EXPLICIT THAN PIP. SO, I CALLED MYSELF PIP, AND CAME TO BE CALLED PIP.

I give Pirrip as my father's family name, on the authority of his tombstone and my sister — Mrs. Joe Gargery, who married the blacksmith. As I never saw my father or my mother, and never saw any likeness of either of them (for their days were long before the days of photographs), my first fancies regarding what they were like, were unreasonably derived from their tombstones. The shape of the letters on my father's, gave me an odd idea that he was a square, stout, dark man, with curly black hair. From the character and turn of the inscription, "Also Georgiana Wife of the Above," I drew a childish conclusion that my mother was freckled and sickly. *TO FIVE LITTLE STONE LOZENGES, EACH ABOUT A FOOT AND A HALF LONG, WHICH WERE ARRANGED IN A NEAT ROW BESIDE THEIR GRAVE, AND WERE SACRED TO THE MEMORY OF FIVE LITTLE BROTHERS OF MINE — WHO GAVE UP TRYING TO GET A LIVING, EXCEEDINGLY EARLY IN THAT UNIVERSAL STRUGGLE — I AM INDEBTED FOR A BELIEF I RELIGIOUSLY ENTERTAINED THAT THEY HAD ALL BEEN BORN ON THEIR BACKS WITH THEIR HANDS IN THEIR TROUSERS-POCKETS, AND HAD NEVER TAKEN THEM OUT IN THIS STATE OF EXISTENCE.*

Ours was the marsh country, down by the river, within, as the river wound, twenty miles of the sea. My first most vivid and broad impression of the identity of things, seems to me to have

Sueh Li Tan
b1981/Malaysia
www.suehlitan.com

I have typeset my opening page of
Great Expectations in several fonts to draw
a distinction between passages of the story
and heighten the experience of reading
the opening of this classic novel.

The heading, Chapter 1, is set in Gill Sans
Light Shadowed, announcing the opening of
the novel. The first paragraph is in Gill Sans
Light to reflect the honest and open tone
as Pip begins his story. As Pip introduces
his father, sister and her husband, and his
mother and five little brothers, the typefaces
change to reflect what I have understood
of the characteristics of these people.

Following this 'unconventional' way of
starting the chapter, I have used the less
obtrusive Caslon to quietly lead the reader
into the story that follows.

Gill Sans Light Shadowed
Monotype
Eric Gill, 1931

Gill Sans Light
Monotype
Eric Gill, 1931

Bureau Grotesque Three Seven
Font Bureau
David Berlow, 1989–1993

Joanna Italic
Monotype
Eric Gill, 1937

Balloon BT Bold
Bitstream
Max R Kaufmann, 1939

Adobe Caslon Pro Regular
Carol Twombly, 1990
after William Caslon, 1725

Tim Hutchinson Design

My father's family name being Pirrip, and my christian name Philip, my infant tongue could make of both names nothing longer or more explicit than Pip. So, I called myself Pip, and came to be called Pip.

I give Pirrip as my father's family name, on the authority of his tombstone and my sister—Mrs. Joe Gargery, who married the blacksmith. As I never saw my father or my mother, and never saw any likeness of either of them (for their days were long before the days of photographs), my first fancies regarding what they were like, were unreasonably derived from their tombstones. The shape of the letters on my father's, gave me an odd idea that he was a square, stout, dark man, with curly black hair. From the character and turn of the inscription, "Also Georgiana wife of the Above," I drew a childish conclusion that my mother was freckled and sickly. To five little stone lozenges, each about a foot and a half long, which were arranged in a neat row beside their grave, and were sacred to the memory of five little brothers of mine—who gave up trying to get a living, exceedingly early in that universal struggle—I am indebted for a belief I religiously entertained that they had all been born on their backs with their hands in their trousers-pockets, and had never taken them out in this state of existence.

Ours was the marsh country, down by the river, within, as the river wound, twenty miles of the sea. My first most vivid and broad impression of the identity of things, seems to me to have

Tim Hutchinson Design
www.timhutchdesign.com

Tim Hutchinson
b1969/UK

I approached *Page 1* by conducting a series of typographic experiments exploring hierarchy. My aim was to visually represent and evoke life's ebb and flow, its daily vicissitudes, its rhythms and pulse, all of which are reflected in *Great Expectations*.

I chose to set each letter of the text to ensure that no two adjacent characters were in the same point size. This meant that each adjoining character was a different height so the word spacing also had to be adjusted relatively.

The final result changes the experience of reading. While the text remains readable in a traditional sense, the looping and warping perspective of the words shifts the emphasis of the language in unexpected ways. To me, my design for *Page 1* is a visual articulation of the notion that nothing is constant. Were it applied to the whole book, it would be possible to use this approach to place emphasis on the text more intentionally.

Univers 55 Roman
Linotype,
originally Deberny & Peignot
Adrian Frutiger, 1957
size variable

Alexander Boxill

CHAPTER 1

My ███
██
██
██████

██
██
██
██
██
██
██
██
██
██
██
██
██
████ struggle ████████████████████ I ████████████████
██
██
██████████████████.

██
██
██

Alexander Boxill
www.alexanderboxill.com

Violetta Boxill
b1970/UK

The individual has always had to struggle
to keep from being overwhelmed by
the tribe. If you try it, you will be lonely
often, and sometimes frightened.
But no price is too high to pay for the
privilege of owning yourself.

F Nietzsche

as the Collins Classics edition, 2010
Kalix
Regular and Italic
Linotype
Franko Luin, 1994
8/9.8pt

Kathryn Cross

longer ... ... thing Pip. So, I called myself Pip, and came to be called Pip.

I give Pirrip as my father's family name, on the authority of his tombstone and my sister – Mrs. Joe Gargery, who married the blacksmith. As I never saw my father or my mother, and never saw any likeness of either of them (for their days were long before the days of photographs), my first fancies regarding what they were like, were unreasonably derived from their tombstones. The shape of the letters on my father's, gave me an odd idea that he was a square, stout, dark man, with curly black hair. From the character and turn of the inscription, "Also Georgiana Wife of the Above," I drew a childish conclusion that my mother was freckled and sickly. To five little stone lozenges, each about a foot and a half long, which were arranged in a neat row beside their grave, and were sacred to the memory of five little brothers of mine – who gave up trying to get a living, exceedingly early in that universal struggle – I am indebted for a belief I religiously entertained that they had all been born on their backs with their hands in their trousers-pockets, and had never taken them out in this state of existence.

Ours was the marsh country, down by the river, within, as the river wound, twenty miles of the sea. My first most vivid and broad impression of the identity of things, seems to me to have

Kathryn Cross
b1988/UK
www.kathryncross.co.uk

BA Graphic Design student
University of Brighton
UK

Great Expectations is a *Bildungsroman*:
a genre of novel in which the focus is on
the growth and development of the main
character from childhood through to
maturity. Typically, in works of this nature,
the character faces a slow and difficult
journey and the answers they seek are
revealed gradually. This notion is reflected
in my *Page 1* design in the way the type
gradually becomes legible through the white
gradient. I chose to use the font Bodoni,
originally designed at the very end of the
eighteenth century and developed
throughout the nineteenth.

Bodoni Std Book
Morris Fuller Benton for
American Type Founders, 1910
after Giambattista Bodoni c1790
9/9.5pt

Chapter I

My father's family name being Pirrip,
and my christian name Philip, my
infant tongue could make of both
names nothing longer or more
explicit than Pip. So, I called myself
Pip, and came to be called Pip.

I give Pirrip as my father's family
name, on the authority of his
tombstone and my sister — Mrs. Joe
Gargery, who married the blacksmith.
As I never saw my father or my
mother, and never saw any likeness
of either of them (for their days were
long before the days of photographs),
my first fancies regarding what they
were like, were unreasonably derived
from their tombstones. The shape of
the letters on my father's, gave me an
odd idea that he was a square, stout,
dark man, with curly black hair. From
the character and turn of the
inscription, "Also Georgiana Wife of
the Above," I drew a childish
conclusion that my mother was
freckled and sickly. To five little stone
lozenges, each about a foot and a
half long, which were arranged in a
neat row beside their grave, and were
sacred to the memory of five little
brothers of mine — who gave up
trying to get a living, exceedingly
early in that universal struggle — I
am indebted for a belief I religiously
entertained that they had all been
born on their backs with their
hands in their trousers-pockets,
and had never taken them out in
this state of existence.

MO-Design
www.mo-design.co

Chao Sioleong
b1978/China

Hong Chong Ip
b1977/China

In our layout for *Page 1*, we tried to express the stages of the novel's storyline. Our design depicts Pip's life. It shows, via typographic experiment, Pip's journey as he is forced to completely reassess his assumptions and rebuild his life.

ITC Symbol Medium
Aldo Novarese, 1984

Chapter heading
26pt

Body text
7/10pt

Pip sits in a cemetery, he is a young orphan living with his sister, and her husband, Joe Gargery, in the marshes of kent. An escaped convict grabs him and orders him to help, his compliance and following guilt is a theme echoed throughout the book.

When introduced to an eccentric old lady he meets the beautiful (and cruel) Estella whom he falls in love with, he dreams of becoming a wealthy gentleman so he might be worthy of her. His hopes are dashed – he is apprenticed to Mr Gargery – the village blacksmith.

A secret benefactor bequeaths Pip a large fortune, and he must go to london immediately to begin his education as a gentleman. In london he shows distaste for his former friends and loved ones but continues to long for estella.

The convict, Magwitch, startles Pip by announcing he is the secret benefactor, Magwitch tells Pip he was so moved by his boyhood kindness, he dediCated his life to making him a nobleman.

Pip learns estella had been raised by the old lady to break men's hearts – Pip a mere *b*oy for her to learn on, many years later they meet, her man who treated her in a fou*l* way is now dead. Pip sees she is now with remorse, they go together, hand in hand.

Playing on the idea of expectations
and combining this with our role as both
designers and curators of information,
we have broken down the text of *Page 1*
to create a synopsis of the book.

The brief asked that we use the text from
the first page of the Collins edition of the
novel. Encapsulating our desire to simplify
the communication of complex ideas, we
limited ourselves to using only the characters
that appeared in this text. However, not
all were needed to write our synopsis.
The letters and punctuation we found to
be superfluous were:

"kkkkkdeeeeeeeeeeeeeeeeeeeeeeeeez
mmmmmmmmmmmmmmmnnnnnnnnnn
hhhhxxxvvvvvvvvvvvvuuttttttttttttttttttttttttttt
ttttttttt1iiiiiiiiiiiiiiiiiiiiii/sssssfffffffffffffffffffffff
ggoooooooooooyyyyyyyyyyyyyyywwwwwww
,,,,,,,,,aaaaaaaaaaaaaaaaaaaaaaaaaarrrrrrr
rrrrrrrrrrrrrrrrrrrrrrrrrrrrrrrrAAFIIIIIORSTT""

The result, we hope, is a succinct
abridgement of the novel.

The text has been classically set using
Monotype's Fournier; a revival of a typeface
that originated in France during the
eighteenth century.

Fournier
Regular and Italic
Monotype
Monotype Type Drawing Office, 1924
after Pierre Simon Fournier, c1742
11/13pt

Paulus M. Dreibholz
Atelier for Typography and Graphic Design

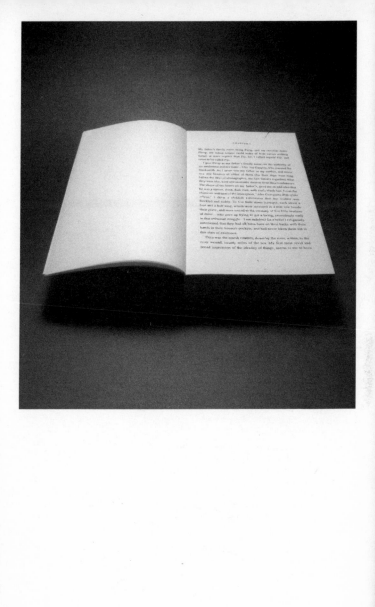

Paulus M. Dreibholz
Atelier for Typography and Graphic Design
www.dreibholz.com

Paulus Dreibholz
b1977/Austria

Before you begin to read a text, or
even before you see a page, you see a book:
a three-dimensional object. As a reader
you 'read' the object, you measure it up,
anticipate its weight, its texture, its smell, and
consider the way it will behave in your hands
before picking it up or leafing through it.

From the object's physical characteristics –
the materials, colours and finishing
techniques – a reader also anticipates the
nature of its content. Books don't come
in a 'standard size' but are shaped by
designers, audiences, methods of production
and distribution and the wider culture of
reading. Books are an integral part of our
every day and have their own vocabulary and
grammar. Readers have come to understand
this language.

Once it has been inspected as an object,
a reader holds the book and *sees* the letters,
their shapes, their density and hierarchies,
and their relation to the page and to the book
as a whole. All this happens, consciously
and unconsciously, before a reader begins
to *read* the letters, words, text, content.

The outline of a shadow betrays the object
that has cast it, so the book leads the reader
to have certain expectations; sometimes
great ones.

The photograph features a book made
to the exact measurements of the one
you are currently holding in your hands
but containing the exact number of pages
of the first edition of Charles Dickens'
Great Expectations. The 'body' of this
codex disappears in the darkness of the
high-contrast photograph, leaving only
the shadow to hint at its physicality.

Astrid Stavro

CHAPTER I

My father's family name being Pirrip, and my christian name Philip, my infant tongue could make of both names nothing longer or more explicit than Pip. So, I called myself Pip, and came to be called Pip.

I give Pirrip as my father's family name, on the authority of his tombstone and my sister – Mrs. Joe Gargery, who married the blacksmith. As I never saw my father or my mother, and never saw any likeness of either of them (for their days were long before the days of photographs), my first fancies regarding what they were like, were unreasonably derived from their tombstones. The shape of the letters on my father's, gave me an odd idea that he was a square, stout, dark man, with curly black hair. From the character and turn of the inscription, "*Also Georgiana Wife of the Above*," I drew a childish conclusion that my mother was freckled and sickly. To five little stone lozenges, each about a foot and a half long, which were arranged in a neat row beside their grave, and were sacred to the memory of five little brothers of mine – who gave up trying to get a living, exceedingly early in that universal struggle – I am indebted for a belief I religiously entertained that they had all been born on their backs with their hands in their trousers-pockets, and had never taken them out in this state of existence.

Ours was the marsh country, down by the river, within, as the river wound, twenty miles of the sea. My first most vivid and broad impression of the identity of things, seems to me to have

Astrid Stavro
b1972/Spain
www.astridstavro.com

Boustrophedon is a form of bidirectional text
seen in ancient manuscripts and inscriptions.
Every other line is flipped or reversed, as are
the letters within it. Using boustrophedon for
the *Page 1* text creates the feeling of a river
or flowing water. It represents Pip tracing and
recollecting his life from the beginning to the
end of the story, allowing the reader to feel
the flow of his journey – from his hometown
in Kent, then to London and back again to
Kent, where the story ends.

Caslon 540
Roman, Italic and Small Caps
American Type Founders, 1902
after William Caslon, 1725
8.5/12.5pt

Vivóeusébio

GREAT EXPECTATIONS
Chapter I

y

Vivóeusébio
Portugal
www.vivoeusebio.com

expectation (noun)

1 the act or state of expecting or the state of being expected

2 (usually plural) something looked forward to, whether feared or hoped for

3 an attitude of expectancy or hope; anticipation [1]

Instead of focusing on the graphic designer's usual concerns of grid, font and type size choices when setting up the layout for a new book, we've responded to the *Page 1* challenge by exploring what the first page of a novel can represent for the reader; a moment when they confirm their expectations of the story.

Dealing with this Dickens' classic, we've chosen to follow its title and theme by emphasising Pip's great expectations and delaying the reader's. In order to achieve this we left out every word of the text except the first word: 'My'.

Glossary
grid

[1]
www.thefreedictionary.
com/expectation

Adobe Caslon Pro
Carol Twombly, 1990
after William Caslon, 1725

Bob Wilkinson

was

rly b

stian nam

make of

er or more

hyself Pip

er 1

like   what they were

he was a square, stout, dark ma
curly black hair. From the char
turn of the inscription, "Also Ge
Wife of the Above," I drew a chil
conclusion that my mother was
and sickly. To five little stone lo
each about a foot and a half lon
were arranged in a neat row bes
grave, and were sacred to the m
of five little brothers of mine – w
trying to get a living, exceedingl
n that universal struggle – I am
for a belief I religiously entertain

Great expectations for i

river wound, twen
t most vivid and
identity of things,

face

English Literature

Context

Page: 1 2 3 4

The 19th-century

The key social and cu

1. **Ambition**
   In 1859, Samuel
   if they worked h
   was the age of th

2. **Social class**
   In Victorian time
   or even upper, m
   were expected to
   content in their 's

efi

Zoom – | Zoom +

-4- | -5- | -6- | -7- | -8- | -9- | -1
| -18- | -19- | -20- | -21- | -22- |
- | -30- | -31- | -32- | -33- | -34-
| -42- | -43- | -44- | -45- | -46-
- | -54- | -55- | -56- | -57- | -58-
s Biography

**Charles Dickens - **
Charles John Huffam Di
the Victorian period. Dic
en.wikipedia.org/wiki/Ch

**Charles Dickens - **
24 Sep 2011 ... Charles
collection of works.
www.online-literature.cor

BBC - History - Cha
Read a biography about
(e.g. Great Expectations
www.bbc.co.uk/.../dicke

David Perdue's Cha
Dedicated to Bringing th
charlesdickenspage.co

Images for charles c

30 years experience h
find true love.

amily name being Pirrip, and m
ould make of both names nothi

Bob Wilkinson
b1970/UK

Sometimes I long for empty space, but it is hard to find and even harder to maintain. The busyness of life fights for our attention. More choices, more decisions, more stuff, but less time to think and process things properly. A simple page of black text printed on white paper seems almost like a thing of the past. The way we transmit and receive our stories is changing. Technology is impacting heavily upon how and what we read.

My design for *Page 1* began life as a simple piece of typography. I was determined to apply my modernist principles to achieve clarity, legibility and impact. A grid was created, a typeface and size chosen and text ranged left within a narrow column – but then something unexpected happened. I became aware of my own interference with the text. Even though my decision making appeared rational it was in fact swayed by my personal tastes, bias and cultural background.

I thought about the story itself, about its context and author. I began exploring and became sidetracked. There was too much information, some of it relevant, some not, but all leading me in different directions, calling for my attention and taking up valuable headspace. I tried going back to those comforting, neutral, 'universal' principles, but it was too late.

Glossary
grid

Before I knew it, I was imposing my personal interpretation of the text upon the reader. I was exploring scale and the layers of linked information that lead, assist and distract us in new media, as well as trying to reflect the isolation and separation of Pip, and his feelings as he looks at his parents' gravestone.

I have left little or no room for others to see the original text. My hand is very firmly upon the piece, directing the reading of the text so that readers can only see it my way.

Glossary

Rob Banham
Department of Typography & Graphic Communication
University of Reading
UK

counter
Any fully or partially enclosed space in a character (eg in o and n).

cut
[as in type]
Variant designs of the same typeface (in metal type every size required a different 'cut' and the design needed subtle adjustments for different sizes).

diphthong
A single character formed from two vowels joined together to represent a compound vowel (eg œ).

Doric
[type]
Name given by some type foundries to their Grotesque types.

double-/single-storey
[character]
Single-storey characters are those which follow the handwritten forms of a and g. They appear more frequently in italic than in Roman and are often used in typefaces for children (they are sometimes called infant characters). Most typefaces use the double-storey forms.

drop capital
A large initial capital, two or more lines high, at the beginning of a chapter or paragraph.

folio
In book design this usually refers to the printed page number. It can also refer to the page itself or the format of a book (a folio book is comprised of sheets which are folded in half to create four pages).

French Renaissance Antiqua
[type]
Alternative term to describe Old Face types. Antiqua is used in some countries to refer to Roman types.

grid
Underlying structure used to organise the layout of illustrated or multi-column books.

Grotesque
[type]
Style of sans serif type from the nineteenth century and the first decade of the twentieth century (eg Franklin Gothic). Less monolinear and geometric than sans serif types of the 1920s and 1930s (eg Futura). Also used more generally as an alternative to sans serif.

gutter
The space between columns of text or between facing pages.

humanist sans serif
Style of sans serif type with thick and thin strokes modelled on the proportions of Old Style type (eg Gill Sans).

kerning
In metal type, allowing part of a letter to overhang the body so that it can fit more closely to its neighbour; in film and digital type, a change to spacing between two specific characters.

leading

The space between lines of type. Originally this meant additional spacing material, made from strips of lead, placed between lines of metal type (type with no leading was 'set solid'). Now used to refer to the distance between baselines (line spacing).

ligature

Single characters comprising two or more characters combined. Usually these characters are ones in which the spacing is awkward when they appear next to each other (eg ff/ff). Some types have ligatures for other combinations, such as ct and st.

line-break

Either the simple end of a line within continuous setting, with no semantic significance, or the deliberate ending of a line to indicate the end of a paragraph or a line of poetry.

Modern
[type]

Style of Roman type with vertical stress (the thin parts of the O are at 12 and 6 o'clock), high contrast between thick and thin strokes, and very thin serifs which are often completely horizontal and unbracketed. First introduced at the end of the eighteenth century (eg Bodoni).

Old Face
[type]

Style of Roman type with diagonal stress (the thin parts of the O are at roughly 10 and 4 o'clock), low contrast between thick and thin strokes, and bracketed serifs that are much heavier than in Modern types (eg Bembo). First introduced at the end of the fifteenth century.

Roman
[type]

Serif types based largely on humanist scripts (as opposed to those based on blackletter scripts). Also used to refer to the 'regular' weight of a typeface family.

serif/sans serif

Serifs are the small horizontal or oblique strokes that are added to the basic letterform in Roman typefaces (eg at the either end of the crossbar and at the foot of a capital T). Sans serif, as the name suggests, are types that do not have serifs.

swash
[character]

Swash characters are characters with calligraphic flourishes. Some typefaces come with alternative swash characters that can be substituted for the regular forms. Usually there are alternate forms for just a few characters (eg Garamond Premier Pro) but some typefaces offer a huge number (eg Zapfino).

Transitional
[type]

Style of Roman type between Old Face and Modern (eg Baskerville). This was first introduced at the end of the seventeenth century.

Biographies

Lucienne Roberts

Lucienne Roberts is a graphic designer, writer and co-founder of GraphicDesign&. Her studio, LucienneRoberts+, specialises in design for the public and arts sectors. She was a signatory of the *First Things First 2000* manifesto, which called for greater design responsibility, and has taught at academic institutions in the UK and abroad including Yale and ESAD, Porto. LucienneRoberts+ design projects include: exhibition design for the British Museum and Wellcome Collection; identities for David Miliband's leadership campaign and AVA Academia; and book design for the Design Museum and Panos London. Lucienne's books include *The Designer and the Grid* (2002, Rotovision) and *Good: An Introduction to Ethics in Graphic Design* (2006, AVA Academia).

Rebecca Wright

Rebecca Wright is a design educator, writer and co-founder of GraphicDesign&. She is Academic Director of Communication Design and Course Director of BA (Hons) Graphic Design at Kingston University, London. She gained her MA in illustration from the Royal College of Art and has lectured, spoken at events and acted as consultant at academic institutions across the UK and abroad, including Berlin, Cape Town and Treviso. Her writing on design and design education has been published in numerous books and journals and she is chair and speaker for an annual art and design education programme at the Institute of Education, London. She is currently writing a book on research methods in graphic design for Laurence King Publishing.

Lucienne and Rebecca co-wrote *Design Diaries: Creative Process in Graphic Design* (2010, Laurence King Publishing).

Robert Patten

Professor Robert Patten is Lynette
S Autrey Professor of Humanities at
Rice University, Texas, where he
teaches courses in nineteenth-century
British literature and art, the European
novel, and the history of the book.
He is the author of many books,
including *Charles Dickens and
His Publishers* (Oxford University
Press, 1978) and *Dickens and 'Boz'*
(Cambridge University Press, 2012),
and has been president of the
Society for the History of Authorship,
Reading and Publishing. He has
held Fulbright, Guggenheim and NEH
fellowships and been a fellow at the
National Humanities Center and the
Center for Advanced Study in the
Visual Arts at the National Gallery of
Art, Washington, DC. Professor Patten
is the current Scholar in Residence at
the Charles Dickens Museum, London.

Thank you

to all our design
contributors, who
gave their time, ideas
and expertise far more
generously than we
had any right to ask

and

Professor Robert Patten
Caroline Walmsley
John McGill
Adam Cohen
Rob Banham
Caroline Roberts
Lorna Fray
Emma King
Michael Czerwinski
Andrew Cochrane
John Greager

The very helpful
team at CPI

Kingston University,
London, UK

and

to our families who
have supported us in
setting up what we
hope will be a long and
compelling endeavour:

Damian Wayling
Katy Roberts-Wayling
Ray Roberts

Lawrence Zeegen
Patrick Wright
Judy Wright